A Childhood
in a Welsh
Mining Valley

A Childhood in a Welsh Mining Valley

VIVIAN JONES

with Foreword by
Professor Hywel Francis

y Lolfa

First impression: 2017

© Vivian Jones and Y Lolfa Cyf., 2017

Cover design: Y Lolfa

ISBN: 978 1 78461 375 4

Published and printed in Wales
on paper from well-maintained forests by
Y Lolfa Cyf., Talybont, Ceredigion SY24 5HE
website www.ylolfa.com
e-mail ylolfa@ylolfa.com
tel 01970 832 304
fax 832 782

Contents

Foreword

THE ONLY TIME I ever heard Vivian Jones speak in public, he had a profound effect upon me. Indeed it was quite startling for me and the whole gathering. It was at the top of the Dulais Valley in Onllwyn, 35 years ago, in the local Congregational chapel where he had been a young minister and where my grandfather had been a deacon for many decades. He was one of three Ministers officiating at the packed funeral of our much respected local doctor, Dafydd Aubrey Thomas, who was widely known to have been an atheist. Vivian Jones stunned us all by saying that he and the good doctor shared the same faith, there was a pause, and he then said, 'What we call "honest doubt".'

I remember discussing this with my late father, who shared Dr Thomas' radical politics. He was at the time a leader of the miners' union in South Wales and was with me at the funeral. His own values had been shaped as a boy at this very chapel. The words have remained with me down the decades. Reading this book has finally confirmed my initial instincts. Like every good book there is a phrase somewhere in it which sums up the essence of what it is about. With this fine autobiography you will find it at the very end. He describes himself simply as 'the son of a miner' to explain the kind of man he became. Hewn from the same rock, or more appropriately the same coal seam, Dr Thomas and our one-time Minister were the sons of Welsh mining communities and as a consequence shared the same world-view.

All three would have endorsed today's progressive discourse, summed up as 'we are far more united than the things that divide us'. No doubt, without any irony intended, they would have said 'Amen' to that.

The autobiography is a graphic explanation of how his

family and community roots in the Amman Valley in the rural Welsh-speaking anthracite coalfield of West Wales created his reflective outlook, what he calls 'my basic philosophy for living' which 'shaped my ends'. These were the origins of his 'radical bent', his 'community spirit' and his concern for individual integrity, and which ultimately gave him the courage to acknowledge his honest doubt.

I remember reading that the art critic John Berger passed judgement on the Polish refugee Josef Herman, who settled in Ystradgynlais in the Swansea Valley. Berger erroneously criticised Herman for painting miners as peasants, not as proletarians. He was wrong, at least about the rural anthracite coalfield. Here was a community based on thrift, on resourcefulness, living close to the land as they did, with their smallholdings or big gardens, their chickens and pigs, their love of horse riding, shooting and fishing. Not in any way an urban, heavily-populated environment, this was a society shaped by the Welsh language and an ancient adherence to learning, with only some of the features of modernity: the cinema, the Italian café, children's comics and that emerging secular centre, the Workmen's Hall.

The underlying theme of this autobiography is the seemingly understated pride in the integrity and decency of the people and their culture, but it shines through with the strength of the narrative through the powerful descriptions of family, work and community life which created strong bonds of fellowship and solidarity in an era long before the divisive and fractured consumer society of today.

I remember travelling many times with my father to the Amman Valley in the course of undertaking his trade union, essentially pastoral, work. He had a great affinity with these communities because of their Welshness, their political radicalism, their adherence to their union and their deep cultural hinterland, whether it was their love of learning or their love of rugby. He would always point out the place where the anthracite miners' union was founded, in the Tregib Arms in Brynamman in 1891, and that their rule book was entirely in Welsh. And we would always call to see his friends Martha and Evan Phillips in Garnant. They had lost their only child Gerwyn in the Second World War – serving in the RAF, he never returned from a bombing raid over Germany. Evan had played for Llanelli against the invincible All Blacks in the 1920s: he was as much a local legend then as Shane Williams is today.

Vivian Jones' principle motivation in writing this autobiography was to give an account of his humble yet proud Welsh origins for his American congregation, which he served faithfully from 1980 until 1995. He has done a great service to them, to his family and to his own community in the Amman Valley. Nearly 100 years ago, a very similar young man – an American, Powers Hapgood – visited the Amman Valley. Robert Bussel produced an illuminating biography, *From Harvard to the Ranks of Labor: Powers Hapgood and the American Working Class* (Pennsylvania State University Press, 1999).

In many ways, this validated the childhood experiences of Vivian Jones. Bussel wrote, 'In Ammanford, Wales, he saw a "mining community at its best"... "I am learning a great deal from these 'intellectual' miners".'

I too have learnt from them, from my very first university evening class at Glanamman Workmen's Hall in 1975. I learnt too from playing against Amman United RFC (always losing), from whom I learnt their club song, 'Roll along, Amman United, roll along'.

I have learnt most of all from Vivian Jones' memoir. It truly is a legacy for all of us, not just for his American congregation. I do hope there will be a sequel, about his life in the Dulais Valley and in the United States, for his Welsh 'congregation'.

Professor Hywel Francis
Crynant, Dulais Valley
February 2017

Introduction

THIS BOOK WAS first written in the United States, and was originally meant for the members of Plymouth Congregational Church in Minneapolis, Minnesota, a church I ministered to from 1980–95. Most of the immigrants to Minnesota came from Scandinavia. Coming from a background so different to the vast majority of them, it seemed fair to me that the congregation I served had a right to know something of the influences that had shaped the mind of the preacher they listened to graciously Sunday after Sunday, so I wrote this book.

I hoped that other Welsh Americans too, old or recent settlers, would enjoy reading about life in an area of Wales in a particular period, possibly even an area with which they might have a special connection. Maybe some of the American public at large might also be interested in my story. Certainly many of them sang Welsh hymn tunes in their churches on Sundays.

But that was a busy time in my life, and although I made time to write the book I didn't get around to talking to a publisher. Now, years later, back on home soil, the book has re-surfaced, and it seems to me that the contents might give to some Welsh people my age the pleasure it has given me of retrieved memories. I would also hope that it would give my children and grandchildren a more rounded view of where they have come from, and that it could help young Welsh people at large to understand a little better how completely the world of some of us has changed in our lifetime. Apart from its vocabulary ('curtains' for 'drapes', etc.) and some forms of spelling (e.g. 'honour' for 'honor'), it has needed little change. It seemed natural when I wrote the book to make the many references I made to the US, and I have decided to let those stand. But I hope the book makes it clear that although I have used an autobiographical format, the book is not about me, but about the valley of my childhood.

The name of the river and valley I have written about is variously spelt as Aman and Amman. I have followed as best I can the spellings on the current road signs and maps.

I'd like to dedicate the book to a selection – it could easily have been a longer list – of American friends who helped my wife and I feel at home in their land: Terry and Ruth Hanold, Ann and David Buran, Mim and Dave Hanson, Dave and Ruth Waterbury, Doug and Mary Jones, Jack and Ann Cole, Philip and Carolyn Brunelle, Fouad and Nancy Azzam, plus an incomparable soul who honoured me with his rich friendship years ago when he was my fellow-student in Princeton in the States, and who still makes a difference in my life: Dr Joe Mullin, a retired Presbyterian minister now living in Greensboro, North Carolina – Joe.

Thanks go to Mary my wife always, for filling my days with taste and colour; to my intelligent daughters, Anna and Heledd, for their friendship; and my four bright and good-looking

Vivian Jones with his wife, Mary

grandchildren, Lowri, Samuel, Manon and Dyfan, for keeping me in touch with the gadgets of the modern world!

It has also been a pleasure meeting Lefi and Garmon Gruffudd of Y Lolfa, while the kind advice of Carolyn Hodges, English-language editor at Y Lolfa, has improved the book in many ways.

Vivian Jones
February 2017

Chapter 1

My Valley

WHEN A MAN reaches 50, wrote a Welsh poet (in Welsh), he can see fairly clearly the place and the people that have moulded his life.

Well past the 50 mark now, I can see that the soil in which my sense of belonging struck its earliest and deepest roots, the terrain whose physical features imprinted indelibly on my young mind images of great natural beauty and some of my basic metaphors for living, the square mile whose boundaries first provoked in me a wonder about how green the grass might be elsewhere, is one of the old industrial valleys in the south of 'the cramped womb' that is little Wales.

The old industrial valleys of South Wales are not in any major league of the world's valleys for size. They are not Colorado Valleys or Danube Basins, let alone Great Rift Valleys visible from outer space. Like children's stories, their beginnings and endings are not far from each other, and their slopes, like trained collies, closely shepherd the rain-fed, fast-flowing rivers that scoured them into being and bestowed on them their names. Insignificant though they may be now in the eyes of the outside world, in their heyday those modest, unassuming, rough, tough valleys were suppliers of vast amounts of coal of the highest quality, and almost equivalent amounts of metals, even to the most distant corners of the world.

The similarity of the social and political and religious life which grew out of the similar physical and industrial and economic conditions which prevailed in these Valleys once, created out of the lives of their inhabitants a shared, proletarian, exuberant culture that gave to all these valleys together a new and singular and assertive identity. So it is that, although Wales has other valleys, some of them of great beauty, when the Welsh speak of 'the Valleys', they mean this erstwhile boisterous, pulsating chorus of valleys in the industrial south. For people outside of Wales, in England especially, the stereotypical Welshman became (and in the minds of some continues to be, for better or for worse) the product of this culture. The phrase 'the Valleys' – as if it were linked to a time-warp – is still enshrouded in an aura of that comparatively recent past, in shades of the riot of singing and suffering, of passion and politics, of rugby and religion, of pathos and poetry that exploded when Coal became King.

I know now too that the people who have moulded my life, who have 'shaped my ends', came from a community in one of those valleys that 'took me in from the void of unbeing', to quote R S Thomas, another Welsh poet (who wrote in English). It was the community in that one valley which imparted to me the ambiguities that polarise my existence – my brash humour and my insecurity, my mix of both pride and humility, my idealism and my cynicism, my radical bent and my fear of what others may think, my community spirit and my concern for individual integrity.

That one valley, the Amman Valley, is the beginning of the western rim of the South Wales coalfield. In the eastern valleys, it was steam coal, or soft coal, that was mined. The western rim is an area where anthracite, or hard coal, was mined. Miners in the western hard-coal valleys tended to be a little more independent than miners in the eastern valleys. A visible sign of that difference was the number of self-owned, large, detached houses in the western valleys, as contrasted with the typically small, terraced houses rented from the mine owners in the eastern valleys.

The River Amman, which created my valley and gave it its name, the Amman Valley (in Welsh *Cwm Aman*), is, judging by the stones in its bed, a very young river. It has its source on the slope of the Black Mountain to the east. From there it flows some eight miles and merges in the village of Pantyffynnon with the River Loughor. The resultant flow is called the Loughor River, and so there the River Amman and Cwm Aman come to an end.

Life in a valley shares features with life in other valleys, of course: valleys people live under a smaller canopy than people who live on plains, and that can have consequences – it often leads to a much higher degree of social interaction. But a valley can have distinctive characteristics too. The Amman Valley for instance, is hard done by in some ways. In addition to the fact that there's a village called Cwmaman in a valley to the east, with which it's sometimes confused, it isn't as long as most other Welsh valleys. Ammanford, a pleasant but small and relatively new township which grew along with the development of local coalmines, functions as its 'capital', and is situated a mile or so before it ends, but no ancient or even fairly large town, let alone a city, claims the valley as its hinterland, as Neath does the Neath Valley, or Bridgend the Ogwr Valley, or Newport the Wye Valley. Neither does it have any striking claim to fame: no mighty hymn tune such as Cwm Rhondda has carried its name to the four corners of the earth. No world-renowned diva made her home there, as Madam Adelina Patti made her home at Craig y Nos in the upper reaches of the Swansea Valley, to which she would invite as her guests some of Europe's crowned heads. It hasn't been, like the Afan Valley, the birthplace of such Hollywood stars as Richard Burton and Anthony Hopkins. It doesn't have an ancient ruin that has been immortalised as Wordsworth immortalised Tintern Abbey in the Wye Valley. Mentioning the Amman Valley elsewhere can tend to bring a puzzled look to people's faces, rather than a firm nod of recognition. In a series of Welsh-language volumes on the Valleys, the one on the Amman Valley struggled more than a little – more than was necessary in my view, but that too makes a point.

Yet in other quiet ways the Amman Valley has much going for it. Physically, like other western valleys, it is not as narrow and harsh as most valleys to the east, and its mountains lean to the nurturing rather than the challenging. They are low and laid back rather than steep and dominating; smoothly and gently curved rather than angular and craggy. The valley floor too, is mostly in pleasing proportion to the heights on either side, so that the overall effect is of a comparatively harmonious, although not over-indulgent, Mother Nature.

At one time the valley's industries were a dominating enough factor on the valley floor, and a dominating enough economic and social factor in the daily lives of its inhabitants, for a coal miner's small son, living in the midst of it all, to be able to forget everything else. Despite having classmates who lived on a farm, despite his own contact with farms and nature, and despite a backdrop of mountains, he could forget that there was anything beyond the immediate tips, beyond the machinery used and disused in and around the colliery, beyond the railway sidings, beyond smoke and grime and rivulets muddied by slurry, beyond workers returning from their day's labour with black faces, carrying empty tea cans and sandwich boxes, wearing work-clothes and peaked caps. But in fact, industry in Cwm Aman was not so overwhelming, nor the valley so confined, that there was not enough room also, beyond the reach of industry's sprawl, especially on the valley's lower slopes, for green fields, flowering hedgerows and clear brooks. There were inviting paths and country lanes, picturesque farms and a few smallholdings, with horses, cows and sheep grazing , farmers with weather-beaten cheeks who lived by the seasons and who went to mart wearing corduroy trousers, and farmers' wives with flowered overalls and dimpled elbows, who kept gardens, looked after young calves and sucking lambs and chickens, took small beer out to the fields when the men harvested the hay, and fed their husbands, their sons and daughters too perhaps.

The lie of a land, the way it presents and offers itself, can influence its people. Historians in the United States have wondered how breaking out from forestland to cross the

Mississippi into the open prairie of the Great Plains, where they suddenly found themselves – at least when they were carried on wagons or mounted on horseback – to be the tallest entities in sight on a vast and unbroken sea of tallgrass, affected the psyche of the early American pioneers. After an initial awe, was there an awareness of destiny, a sense of a boundless challenge and a call for an answerable courage? That question hasn't been asked about valley people – they were never the tallest thing in sight on a boundless horizon. Valley people always live, move and have their being hemmed in and overshadowed. Whereas flat land offers a uniform, equitable, light, airy sense of space and headroom, of unrestricted openness, of freedom in all directions, a valley fragments life and contains it, apportioning and shading it in subtle and not-so-subtle ways.

On the other hand, valleys are Nature's art galleries, and their people the viewing public. Their distant surroundings, strikingly beautiful in one way or another, are visually ever-present to people who live in valleys, whereas on a plain, distant scenery can be present only in the mind's eye. Far-off bare mountain-top sheep pastures and fern-covered rises and woods, outlying farms closer by, embraced by clusters of meadows, and houses closer still, all of which would be invisible in flat terrain, are raised dramatically in valleys, so that they can be seen as if from a plane which is banking. Nature in a valley is an extrovert, a blatant and shameless exhibitionist, an artist that offers a free and grand show of her speciality: landscapes. Sometimes I still see my valley through the filter of memories of the industrial past, and then I have to be reminded, perhaps by seeing it through the eyes of a visitor looking at it for the first time, how strangely beautiful it all is, and how cleansing it must be, even at a subconscious level, to have a long visual intimacy with Nature at its loveliest.

Before holidays far afield were the norm, before everyone owned a car, before walking became a hobby for suitably-attired and properly-equipped people with maps and serious inclinations, climbing slopes and hills and mountains was a feature of life in the valleys. We did so to gather blackberries, or to collect hazelnuts, or to visit friends on a hillside farm, or to cross over to the next valley to see distant relatives, or to enjoy the views, or to get away from it all. Ascending the mountains enabled one to see one's valley, one's village, even one's street and one's house, from another perspective, which could sometimes be therapeutic, possibly contributing to a saner outlook on some personal dilemma getting out of hand. A Welshman who became a professor of psychiatry at St Bart's Hospital in London once told me that open public spaces are not a luxury but a necessity in a large city, and that if all the public parks in London were taken away overnight, incidences of mental illness would multiply and overwhelm us. Our mountains were our public parks, except that we felt a greater sense of ownership and freedom in them than Londoners might feel in their measured and manicured parks. We had no signs on our mountains proclaiming that this one was in the Borough of Islington, that one in the Royal Borough of Kensington, or that we would be fined if we picked the flowers, or if dogs weren't kept on a chain, or fouled a footpath.

Our mountains, the protagonists in the visual drama that constitutes a valley, were God's land. The process of getting to know and to love them began early for me, although it was by no means unambiguous initially. Every autumn Mam and Dad would take us up to the heathland on the Black Mountain, on the northern side of our valley; quart milk jugs in their hands and small, unbreakable tin cups for my sister and me. There we would gather the small black, blue-dusted berries that grew on shrubs among the heather and ferns, shrubs which reached upward no more than a foot above the ground. It was a back-breaking chore for adults, but wimberry pie was a great delicacy, and unlike gooseberries or blackberries, wimberries had no seeds to get into anyone's cavities or under anyone's dentures! On one such expedition, absorbed in a little world of my own, I wandered into a patch of ferns that were taller than I was, so that when I looked around I had no idea which direction to

green space [handwritten margin note]

take to return to my parents. I was too little to have wandered far, but not knowing that, I screamed in terror until Dad came to pick me up and comfort me. For a little child, accustomed to small, friendly, enclosed spaces, a mountain was like the sea on a first visit: now a delightful new element in which to play at its edge, happy and carefree; but a few steps too far in and this great sweep without hedge or fence or wall, this boundless expanse, this very edge of one's known and trusted universe, could quickly become intimidating and menacing to a young spirit not yet equipped with enough curiosity and courage to reach out very far.

In time, as childhood became boyhood, all fear of the mountains would be replaced by the welcome familiarity of their dependable solidity, by a comforting sense also of their timelessness. There would be summer memories, and promises too, of space to run and run and run in any direction, before collapsing, exhausted, to lie on one's back on cool, spongy moss or in tinder-dry grass among clumps of heather. Then when the deafening thunder of one's own heartbeat had quietened, one might pick up the distant song of a skylark, and peer upward, shielding one's eyes with one's hands while straining to catch a glimpse of the motionless black speck, high up there somewhere against the white blaze of an August afternoon sun, pouring out its heart, as Shelley once wrote, '…In profuse strains of unpremeditated art.'

Primary natural features, such as seas, deserts, lakes, forests and great rivers, dispose people who must live on their terms to have a deeper understanding of some basic truths than of others, and to understand those truths much better perhaps than other people understand them, as if there were depths within those truths which were their special birthright. Climbing slopes and hills and mountains time and time again imprinted on the psyche and spirit of valley people the correlation between the effort of striving upward and the rewards of completion, of reaching the top. It also offered a different, more detached perspective on familiar things behind and below. If one climbed high enough, one also gained a panoramic view of a distant, larger world. Of course, the experience of coming down again also offered postscripts, and the wary, self-protective mindset of the people of the valleys demanded that they remembered those too. They remembered them well, and they drummed them into the minds of their children long before their children would consciously possess them for themselves – that it is much easier and quicker to descend than to ascend, to go downhill than uphill, to get to the bottom again than it is to reach the top.

Two other factors, the Welsh language, and chapelgoing, both of which reinforced each other, continued to hold sway in the western valleys for a longer time than they did in the eastern valleys. This consequently put something of a brake on the speed of social change there, giving those communities for a time a greater degree of cohesion and a deeper sense of roots. Yet despite (judging by the mundane quality of its literary output) a degree of cultural in-betweenness which has contributed something of an identity problem for the Amman Valley, the bias of its life has been more to the western valleys, and so to the industrial-rural, traditionally-cultured area of Wales, than toward the heavily-industrialised, more culturally-rootless, and eventually more anglicised, valleys to the east.

The complete Amman Valley extends, of course, from the source of the Amman to its junction with the Loughor, but at one time the Amman Valley was the proper name for one particular central stretch of that greater valley, and in common parlance the name oftener than not still refers to that one stretch. Certainly for me as a child, it was this stretch that was my Cwm Aman.

If I had to choose one visible symbol for this Amman Valley, I would have no need to hesitate for a second. Mircea Eliade, a Romanian historian of religion who became a Professor at the University of Chicago, wrote about humanity's 'significant spaces' – the places where people raised their temples or buried

19

their dead. In both of those senses, the most significant space in my Cwm Aman is a small chapel. It stands alone, a solitary sentinel at the top of one of the lower slopes of the northern side of the valley, higher up than any other building at that point except for a farm some distance behind it, and it symbolises much of the history and the ethos of the valley. It's called Hen Bethel. That name has to be the best that could have been given to it, acknowledging affectionately and meaningfully the two cultures in which it is rooted, for Bethel is a composite Hebrew word, *beth* meaning house, and *el* meaning God, while the Welsh *hen* can express belovedness as well as age.

Hen Bethel is the oldest religious site in the valley. It's the womb of the independent and 'democratic' Congregationalism which, with a head start on the other denominations, became the ethos that for a long time shaped the spiritual, moral and cultural life of the valley (and, through the *Mayflower* Pilgrims, and the Mayflower Compact, the ethos that first shaped not only the spiritual, moral and cultural life of New England, but the initial political disposition of the United States). Hen Bethel is a witness to where so many of us who were born and raised within sight of it came from in a deep sense. 'A serious house on serious earth it is', as the English poet Philip Larkin wrote of another religious edifice.

Hen Bethel Chapel on the side of the valley

At the time that small chapel was built, non-Anglicans had been allowed a measure of tolerance on the British religious scene, but the law was still protective of the Anglican Church, and people other than Anglicans had to build their places of worship away from centres of population. In time, however, the population in the valley increased, and the Dissenters who had broken away from the Anglicans and raised Hen Bethel became themselves the religious establishment in Wales. Hen Bethel became too small and too out-of-the-way for its fast-growing congregation, and Bethel Newydd (New Bethel) was built on a raised mound beside the main road on the valley floor. For a long time, Bethel Newydd's members continued to use Hen Bethel for weddings and funerals, and for occasional special services such as one at six o'clock on Christmas morning. This is the only service held there now, and people from near and far still come to it.

Although the members of Bethel Newydd own it, Hen Bethel has long since transcended denominational limitations, even formal religious limitations, so that today it's difficult to think of it as being owned in a conventional sense by a particular group of people. Time and familiarity, plus the stake so many – in a sense the whole community – have in its cemetery, mean that by this time anyone at all in the valley can feel a sense of ownership of Hen Bethel.

The chapel's cemetery lies behind it, and drifts out to one side like a spread-out ankle-length skirt. The gravestones there – the older ones carved from local stone, the newer ones from black, white or brown polished granite, all visible from afar as a salt-and-pepper patch on the hillside – soberly affirm our earthly transience. We are, as our own poet Dylan Thomas has put it, 'all poor creatures born to die', and no matter how long we may live, the days of whatever joys and troubles life bestows on us are numbered. The gravestones affirm too that that mortality binds us together more surely than the strongest possible chain. Yet nowhere is the line between here and the beyond, between this world and the next, between time and eternity, more blurred for me than when I visit Hen Bethel on a warm, still, humming summer's day, and wander alone around the old part of the cemetery, which seamlessly extends the weathered grace of Hen Bethel itself.

I once visited a piece of original North American prairie, just to see it, stand on it and walk around in it. What had aroused a desire in me to do so was a book by a naturalist telling of going himself to look for a particular patch of original prairie grass, and of knowing at one point that he must be close to it, yet being unable to recognise it. Then suddenly he saw it on a hillside in the distance. The sight of that patch of prairie grass, unchanged over centuries but now surrounded by cultivated fields, reminded him, he wrote, of once seeing on another hillside one solitary wild buffalo grazing in the midst of a herd of domestic cattle; dairy cattle that were the products of years of careful breeding. In a valley in which old and antiquated houses are constantly being renewed and modernised and in which new houses are being built, Hen Bethel and its cemetery, clinging to their hillside, remind me of that patch of prairie grass and that buffalo – something that hasn't changed over time and can't be replicated; one of a kind, an original.

A few of the gravestones in Hen Bethel's cemetery bear the names of some of the valley's rich or well-known dead, and tell of themes in the valley's story. The grandest and tallest commemorates a man who toward the end of the nineteenth century left the valley for the United States, settled in New York, became wealthy, then left instructions in his will that when he died his body should be returned to Wales to be buried in Hen Bethel's cemetery. I was a small, very impressionable, seven-year-old boy, my hand held tightly by my mother's, when I stood with the large throng of people that lined the road to watch his oddly-shaped coffin borne in a slow-moving hearse to the dead man's final resting place. The hearse was preceded first by local ministers, then by men who remembered the deceased or knew the family, and it was followed by the remaining male relatives. Although the arrangements locally were in the hands of the village's own carpenter/undertaker, two American funeral directors had accompanied the corpse back from the United States, first across the Atlantic, then overland from Southampton, to our valley. The final, overland stage of the journey alone was beyond the imagination of most of us who had gathered to watch. Our sedate and staid community, ahead of time fascinated by the exotic dimensions of the event, was then to be startled, shocked and offended, even, on seeing the two Americans walk alongside the bible-black, heavy-worsted-suited funeral procession, brazenly wearing sacrilegious, light grey flannel suits. It was, I think, my first cross-cultural experience, my first contact with pluralism!

Ryan's gravestone also lies in Hen Bethel's cemetery now. Ryan, who would be just a little younger than I am today had he lived, and who, like so many young people in the valley, took up the calling of teaching and went away to England to find employment – Wales for decades produced more teachers than it needed. Only later did he find his vocation as an entertainer and return to Wales to sing, create kindly laughter, and win great affection through live concerts and radio and television shows in Welsh or in English, and sometimes in a mixture of both. It was in the United States that he, like Dylan Thomas, died suddenly when not yet quite forty years old. Like Dylan, his body, too, was brought back to be buried in the land which had received him 'out of the void of unbeing' – to quote R S Thomas again.

Hen Bethel's cemetery connects with the stories of living ordinary folk as well, of course, because for many of us the dead in the cemetery are our own. It is their physical and spiritual genes that we carry within us. My maternal grandfather's prostrate memorial lies there, unostentatious but solid, the few lines of well-chosen strict-metre poetry in Welsh about a coal miner in gold-leaf lettering on its black granite, likely to last for a long, long time. I was never close to my paternal grandfather, who lived in the next village, Glanamman. We didn't visit his home often, and he didn't show much interest in me when we did. That might have been because I was his ninth grandchild, his fifth grandson, but I don't know that he showed much interest in any other people at that stage in his life, or ever really perhaps. He was a qualified grandfather, he was 'Tad-cu Glanamman'. However, although I was my maternal grandfather's second grandchild, I was his first grandson, and we as a family lived close to him in more ways than one. He was my Tad-cu.

In the days before cremation, when all the dead were buried, when families were large, when so many people in the Amman Valley were inter-related, when attending funerals was a social obligation, and when most people could expect that it would be their own final resting place too, there was a sense of Hen Bethel's cemetery, despite its detached location, as a hallowed extension of the village, a consecrated place for very many of us to visit reverently from time to time, and together to care for lovingly.

Hen Bethel presides benevolently and with restrained dignity over the valley below it. Its front – two large windows, each flanked by a door, the whitewash on the walls faded, and all topped by a dark slate roof, looks down on the valley like a much-loved old countenance, and its mellow spirit bestows on all who live and pass beneath it a slow blessing as they go on their often hurried way. Living some distance away now, I never drive up or down the Amman Valley without raising my gaze toward the Black Mountain to reassure myself that no matter what troubles may beset me and the world at that moment, Hen Bethel is still there, a faithful witness to unseen things, and I quietly seek and accept its blessing.

The Amman Valley had customs which went back as far as the memory goes, but which have died out now – just one aspect of the frighteningly endless discontinuities which have taken place during my lifetime. Every Whit Monday (the day following Whitsun, or Pentecost Sunday) when I was a child, it seemed as if every family in the valley went on a statutory seven-mile walk, leaving behind them for one whole long day

Hen Bethel Chapel

a ghost valley inhabited only by the sick and the old. The first stage of the walk for the people who lived in our village was across the river, up the hillside past Hen Bethel, then along the road which diagonally climbed the side of the Black Mountain. In baskets and bags and backpacks, Dad and Mam and my sister and I would carry everything needed for lunch and tea, from teacups and plates and cutlery and a teapot and a kettle, through a table-cloth and condiments, to a box of matches. And the food itself, of course. The last thing to happen before we left the house and Dad locked the door, was that loads would be distributed and tested, adjusted or redistributed if necessary, and then we would be away.

Our first stop would be at a grass verge somewhere on the roadside above Hen Bethel cemetery. We children would collect kindling, dad would light a fire, clear water collected by my sister and me from a nearby brook would be boiled in the kettle, and in no time at all Mam would have a lunch prepared for us. We would enjoy it sitting on a blanket laid on the grass. In the fresh air of early summer the meal, whatever it consisted of, would always taste as food never tasted indoors.

We children, enjoying the novelty of eating outdoors, would not only eat without urging from our parents but would even have to be stopped eventually so that there would be enough left for our tea.

As we ate we would be greeted by passers-by, whether they knew us well or not, as if we were royalty and they our courtiers. And in between mouthfuls of food and responding to greetings, Dad would challenge us with questions about the small world behind and below us – and offer prizes. 'How many houses are there on Cowell Road? I'll give half my piece of cake to whoever gets it right first.' He would also draw our attention to things he was himself observing for the first time – 'My goodness, look at the size of Mr Leyshon's house!' (Mr Leyshon was the minister of Bethel Newydd) 'From here it actually looks bigger than Calfaria.' (Calfaria was the Baptist chapel) 'You'd never think that just by passing it, would you?'

When our meal was done and we had packed everything up again, carrying away with us any litter, scattering the ashes of our fire and making sure there were no live embers – and after I had returned from a visit into the bushes – we would continue on, passing and greeting those who had passed and greeted us, as they now sat at the roadside further on, in turn enjoying their lunch.

Higher up on the mountain we would turn aside at one spot to see Llygad Llwchwr just a little way from the roadside. Llygad Llwchwr, or 'Eye of the Loughor', was the source of the River Loughor. Next to the cleft in the rock from which the water issued, there was a large cave. I once climbed inside it on one of those Whit Monday walks and found carved in the rock there the initials DJD. Tad-cu's initials were DJD – for Daniel John Daniel – but I don't remember ever asking him whether the initials in that cave were actually his, and whether he himself had carved them. In a world which contained trillions of questions, dozens of which it was firing at his brain every second, a small boy couldn't possibly be expected to retain any one question for more than an hour or two. But I do remember returning as an adult to Llygad Llwchwr with my wife, and refusing to accept that the small cave next to the cleft from which the Llwchwr emerged was the huge one I had entered as a boy.

When the road reached the top of the Black Mountain, we would begin to descend into another valley. We would now be looking down at a scene free from even a hint of industry, a scene of scattered, whitewashed farms and small hedged fields, every hedge and field a different shade of green, the whole patchwork quilt covering the low hill on the other side and hillsides beyond that as far as the eye could see. Then having reached the base of the valley, we went on to the centre of the valley to climb first a hill and then a steep path that would lead to our final destination, Carreg Cennen Castle: a magnificent, glorious ruined fortress high on a massive rock; as grand, picturesque and dramatic a castle as any child could possibly conceive of.

Inside the castle there were grassy banks on which adults collapsed after the climb, but for an energetic, enthusiastic and imaginative little boy there was no time to relax with such a great deal of tremendous responsibility to assume. There were arrow-slits through which to watch out for any enemy that might suddenly come over the surrounding hills, ramparts to climb and be ready to defend from a possible week-long siege, and turrets to possess and occupy and hold on to until the very last drop of blood.

At one corner of the ruins there was a notorious cave, carved out of the rock and descending quite a way into darkness. At the end of this, at one time, it is said, there was a well from which the denizens of the castle could get water should they be besieged. Some who visited the castle would bring candles or torches to explore the cave. The candles of young men who entered the cave accompanied by their girlfriends tended to be blown out in the still air by totally unexpected and completely inexplicable draughts, or their torch batteries would fail, no matter how new they were. Some shrewd or shy young women

27

invited to go down and explore would cry off, frightened, they would perhaps say, of falling on the wet, slippery rock underfoot.

Afternoon tea would be taken on the grass inside the castle. Then, our loads much lighter, we would begin the homeward journey, more of it downhill than the outward journey. Once, I remember, as the evening wore on, with still some way to go, we were overtaken by a car, a rare occurrence there in those days. The driver, who knew Mam and Dad, and who already had two passengers with him in the car, stopped and kindly offered to give my sister and me a ride as far as Tad-cu's house, where Mam and Dad could pick us up later on the way to our house, a little further on. Not only was I very tired, but no-one in our family owned a car at that point, so a ride in one would have been a great adventure. Dad must have understood that, but even so, after thanking the man, he refused his offer, although letting us go ahead would have been easier for him and Mam too. Dad explained to us after the car had gone that he wanted us all to stay together. Though disappointed, I think I knew even then that it was a learning moment.

Other customs were common to other valleys as well as to ours, but it was in my valley that I encountered them. On New Year's Eve our own young men and women would gather at some meeting point then go around outlying farmhouses to offer New Year greetings by singing New Year songs in Welsh. They would be expected by the farmers and their wives and preparations would have been made for them, and after they had sung and offered their greetings outside, they would be invited inside to be served tea or hot cider, sandwiches and home-baked cakes, in the farmhouse kitchen.

Children did their singing singly on the morning of New Year's Day, but didn't wander as far of course. I would leave the house as soon as it was light, wrapped in a warm coat, a cap on my head, a scarf around my neck knitted by Mam – as were the gloves on my hands. I would go around houses to sing New Year greetings, as did all the other boys in the village, and a few girls who even then refused to be discriminated against, in this matter at least. The songs were mostly well-established ones, but sometimes a local musician might compose a new one, give copies of the words and the music to the parents of some children that he knew, and those parents would teach them to their children. Our songs were in Welsh too, of course. In my prime I had a repertoire of five or six. I would sing one at a dozen or so front doors, then another for a while for a change, and so on. When I had clearly signalled the end of my performance at a particular front door by wishing the inhabitants of the house a Happy New Year through the letter box, someone – perhaps more than one person – would come to the door. If they didn't recognise me, they might ask me whose son I was, then they would wish me too a Happy New Year, and hand me a sum of money. Usually this was a penny or two, sometimes a silver threepenny bit, and should they know my parents, possibly even a silver sixpenny bit. Some people would give me a few sweets, a piece of cake or an apple, and I would make a mental note not to waste time at that house the following year. Even that early in life I understood the advantage of hard currency over perishable goods!

Some thoughtful and practical people, realising how eager I would be to get to as many houses as possible within the time constraints – tradition required that the singing had to stop at midday – came to the door as soon as I began to sing, interrupted my performance, gave me money, told me I needn't sing for them any more, and ushered me quickly on to the next house. Others, with an insular courtesy not harnessed to imagination, and who perhaps, due to an unusually thick front door or possibly a hearing problem, weren't sure they had heard the signing-off good wishes, waited quietly inside until they were absolutely sure you had finished singing. Unfortunately you didn't know that's what was delaying them, so you would begin a second song, and then they would wait till you finished that one too. If your first song had been a new one, at least a few would notice and, curiosity aroused, on coming to the

29

door they might ask you to repeat it while they stood there in front of you, which was a peculiar kind of agony. My parents, concerned with the quality of my performance, and feeling that there should be some clear relationship between the effort I put into it and the rewards I received, were delighted if I had learned a new song for that year, but I saw myself as more in the benevolence than the entertainment business on New Year's Day and so didn't consider composers of new New Year songs among humanity's great benefactors. Because of the time question, it seemed to me that two songs, whether the second was different to the first one or a repeat, deserved twice as much financial reward as one; but it never worked out that way, and I was always puzzled and disappointed that grown-ups couldn't see something so obvious.

If people didn't come to the door and open it after you had sung once and greeted them and it was getting close to midday, and you had already made enough money not to care any more whether you were pleasing your mother by making a reputation as a sweet little boy, you opened the letter box and yelled 'Happy New Year' through it in a tone you hoped sounded sarcastic. You then gave them a few seconds in the hope that you had shamed them into action, and if you hadn't, went on to the next house. Some boys, if they knew someone was inside but not opening the door, and if they had the good luck to have fathers who would do the same in such a circumstance, had less subtle New Year wishes which they (and I) thought suited that situation.

Like most such Valleys communities at that time, many of Cwm Aman's inhabitants were comparatively poor, but it was a poverty alleviated by being an experience shared among so many, and accepted by them. In his 'spiritual journal' *Morning Light*, Jean Sulivan, a French Roman Catholic priest, contrasted today's (Western) poverty with the poverty into which he had been born. 'Today all we have are poor people who have not yet succeeded in getting rich. There was no shame then in being poor. The thousand stings of desire and vanity were foreign to us.' One plus to the shared poverty in the Valleys was that one of society's problems today, security, was hardly a problem. Some people never felt the need to lock the doors of the house, even when there was no-one at home!

The reverse side of the poverty was pride, which was expressed in some societal values. One was independence, a conspicuous feature of life in our valley. A man, for instance, was expected to possess all the tools and spare parts he needed to manage life around his house – to tend his garden, to trim his hedges, to prune his trees, to repair window sashes, to change tap washers, to replace tiles, to point or build walls, to burn off old coats of paint and put on new ones. Borrowing was only for when some tool you owned was broken and you didn't have a replacement part right in the middle of a job, and you needed another one right then because it wasn't a job you could leave unfinished. But the tool was to be returned as soon as the job was finished; cleaned, in good working order and wrapped in a long, apologetic explanation. Women in particular, universally the treasurers in a household, prided themselves on never being in debt, something most of them could ill afford to begin getting into anyway. For some of them that meant never buying anything unless they could pay for it immediately. I recently met an old schoolmate who told me that his mother, who had just died, had to the end of her life adamantly refused to buy anything that involved any kind of deferred payment – or in the vernacular in her day, 'on the never-never!'

There were ways in which needy people in the community were helped toward independence. Miners no longer able to work underground due to some injury suffered at work, the loss of an eye or a leg perhaps, might be given a surface job by a caring manager. Alternatively, they themselves might start a small business on their own, as a cobbler or barber perhaps. Women who were widowed early and had small children to raise might be offered an opportunity to open a post office, or they themselves would open a small store. These small businesses would be carried on in the front room of a house, or in a lean-to shed built on to the side of a house. Other members of the community would go out of their way to support such enterprises, even to the extent of giving them work they might otherwise leave undone, or buying from them things they didn't actually need. 'You never know, that may be just what I might want one day.'

Another practical result of poverty was resourcefulness, a prime and necessary value. Many miners kept chickens, or pigs, or both, and all of them had extensive gardens. Some were competent amateur barbers who took care of haircuts and trims for male or female family members and friends and neighbours, also shaving the men perhaps, or at least trimming their beards and moustaches – a great boon for people confined to their homes due to age or infirmity. And they had the proper tools for the job, those amateur barbers – fine combs and the best hairbrushes, wax spills to singe hair-ends (to prevent colds!), cut-throat razors, but above all, clippers, large and small, which they oiled and cleaned after use as if their lives depended on them, finally wrapping them up well in muslin cloth. Others were amateur cobblers, who would buy leather strips from a market stall in the nearest town. Then with a last, a very sharp knife, a light hammer, small pinhead nails, a file and varnish, they could and would sole and heel the shoes and boots of the whole family. There were dressmakers who not only lengthened existing dresses, took them in, let them out or added a frill or two, making them look like different dresses, but also made new dresses from cloth bought by the customer and brought to them.

It was also a time and place where everything was repaired and re-used many, many times, and nothing at all discarded until it was completely useless. New handles were fitted to old axe-heads, holes in kettles were soldered, children's clothes were patched, screws and nails used once were kept and used again. I remember, in those pre-sellotape days, when a parcel arrived at Tad-cu's house, it would be taken to Tad-cu, and whilst everyone around him would be impatient for him to open it quickly in order to see what was inside, Tad-cu, refusing a scissors or knife if either were offered to him – and hope springing eternal, they usually were – would place the parcel on the kitchen table, slowly untie every single knot in the string which bound it, roll the string up into a ball, and place it in a corner of one of the table drawers, then open out the brown wrapping paper, and fold that carefully before giving it to someone to put away on a shelf in the cupboard to the left of the fireplace. Then, and only then, would he tend to what might be inside the parcel. 'Waste not, want not' was a mantra in Tad-cu's house.

There were also tried and tested home health practices and cure-alls: poultices for blind boils, flannel smeared with goose fat worn next to the chest for a deep cold, camphor oil on muslin worn around the neck for a blocked nose. For extra vitamins to ward off colds in wintertime, children had to pinch their noses and have a lump of sugar in hand to lessen as far as possible the excruciating agonies of tablespoonfuls of evil-smelling and vile-tasting cod liver oil, and for constipation there was the equally evil-smelling and vile-tasting castor oil, syrup of figs, or tea made from senna pods. There were also more people around then who knew what to do when accidents happened than there are in our specialised society today. There was always someone who knew how to apply a tourniquet, or set a bone, or treat someone for shock, or handle a fit of epilepsy. Some people, often following a tradition handed down from generation to generation in a family, performed specialist services necessary in the community at large, such as hedge-laying, building a dry stone wall, baking a wedding cake, delivering a baby, even preparing a body for burial.

In those days, life, of course, was more natural than it is today – closer to the elements, nearer to and more dependent on Nature's rhythms. Children walked long distances to and from school in all weathers. We boys knew, not by studying on the Internet, and not even by virtue of taking a particular interest in the matter, but simply by virtue of being boys, where birds' nests could be found, and we could tell by the nest and its location, and by the eggs in it, the kind of bird that had built the nest. Should we find a nest no one else knew about then it was 'our' nest, to be shown only to our closest friends, and even then only as a great favour and after swearing them to secrecy. Some of us even had contact with a farm, helping a farmer with his milk round on a Saturday morning, or collecting eggs from all over the farm from his free-range chickens, all for a few pence from the farmer (although we would have paid a few pence ourselves for the sense of importance our farm role gave us), and most of us had at least made a few attempts at milking a cow.

When World War II came along and children from the East End of London were evacuated to our part of the country to avoid the German bombing raids, cartoonists had a field day in the local newspapers poking fun at their blissful ignorance of country life. One cartoon, I remember, was of a small boy looking down at a few milk bottles in a field and crying out to his pal, 'Come here quickly, I've found a cow's nest.' (Judging by that scenario, perhaps the cartoonist too was an evacuee.) But my own daughters were in their teens before it dawned suddenly on me one day, as I drove them along a public road that ran through a farmyard, that neither of them had seen a cow being milked!

We were all nourished mostly on garden produce. We had no need then, or perhaps less need, to titillate our palates by eating exotic foods, since so much of our food was seasonal and offered variety, as well as being home-grown and fresh – apart from root vegetables stored for winter, and preserves. Spring meant shallots, lettuce grown under glass, thinnings of carrots, early potatoes and – manna from the gods, the first peas and broad beans, boiled together in a saucepan and eaten from a basin, accompanied by warm fresh bread covered with dollops of melting farmhouse butter! And for dessert, forced rhubarb with custard. Summer was cucumber and beetroot, cabbage and cauliflower, lettuce and carrots and second-early potatoes, and for dessert, strawberries, or gooseberry or blackcurrant tart, with cream – and sometimes, if the van had just passed the house – ice cream (I remember Tad-cu's stunned incredulity when he first encountered what was to him the preposterous idea – 'What on earth is the world coming to!' – of eating ice cream during the winter!). Autumn brought runner beans and marrows, apples, pears, cherries, and the most gloriously-fleshy, sweetest and most succulent of all fruits actually grown or ever dreamed of, Victoria plums – preferably a tad overripe. Winter was the time of soups and broths, of meat and stored vegetables – swedes, parsnips, carrots, old potatoes, and for dessert, apple dumplings and custard, or sweet rice or tapioca or sago. (Exotic fruit such as oranges and bananas and pomegranates were not available the year round, and so a stocking at the foot of the bed stuffed with one of each were a feature of Christmas morning for a child.)

Many vegetables and fruits common all over today weren't available to us then – sweetcorn, peppers, satsumas, courgettes, kiwis. Some years ago an elderly Welsh author, writing of his youth in a rural area of Wales, told of a visit he made to a nearby seaside town with the annual Sunday School trip from his chapel when he was around 20 years old. There he purchased a pound of delicious looking red plums, but discovering they were rotten inside he took them back to the fruiterer's stall, to complain and claim a refund, only to be told by the fruiterer that they weren't plums. They were something he had never before seen or even heard of – tomatoes!

Our lives then were inevitably much less dependent too on gadgets and technology. Refrigerators hadn't arrived, so most houses had a cool dark pantry in which there was a large slate or stone slab on which to place such perishables as bacon and eggs and butter and milk. All those would also be covered with muslin gauze in summer to keep flies away – and sticky fly-catching papers would be hung from the ceilings. Bread was toasted by holding a slice on a long wire fork in front of a grand coal fire – the loveliest winter chore imaginable for children to quarrel over after returning from school soaking wet and cold. There weren't many labour-saving devices in the home – a hand-turned washing machine perhaps, and a mangle, but whereas small boys couldn't be expected to help their mothers wash or wring clothes by hand, they could help with a hand-turned washing machine and a mangle, so human progress wasn't always apparent to me.

During the harvesting season the sweet smell of cut hay hung heavily in the air, and when the time for gathering it came around, even a coal miner like dad helped the farmer who supplied him with milk get his harvest in. He took me with him when I grew older, to hold the reins of the horse that drew the haywain.

Before the coming of the railroad, Cwm Aman had been one sparsely populated place, but the Great Western Railway gave it two stations. Each one needed a separate name, and as the population increased, it was around the two separate foci of those stations that it grew, so that over time Cwm Aman became two separate villages, each identified by the name of its station.

It was from those two neighbouring villages that a poor couple, an unemployed young coal miner who was 22 at the time, and a young woman of 21, went on 31 December 1927 to be married. He had received adult baptism by total immersion as a teenager in Bethesda, the Baptist chapel in the lower village, his village, Glanamman. She had been baptised as a child and confirmed as a teenager in Bethel Newydd in Garnant, her village, the next one up the valley. It was, however, to the Registry Office at Llandeilo some ten miles away that they went to be married, for a registry office wedding would enable them to dispense with some of the costs of a chapel wedding. They returned from their wedding to live in her village, Garnant. Because it was my destiny to be born to this unprepossessing young couple, by making Garnant their home village they also made it my birthplace, and the village where I was to spend my earlier years.

CHAPTER 2

My Village

SOME VILLAGES ARE round, plump as a chicken, with a recognisable centre, while others are scattered around sparsely, with no fixed point, as if the buildings in them had been fired haphazardly out of the proverbial shotgun. Garnant was neither of those kinds. When industry developed in the Valleys and people came from all over to find work, there was a limit to how far sideways any community could expand. But even though our valley was wider than some valleys in South Wales, our village didn't expand sideways as far as it might have, because most people didn't own cars at that time and wanted to live right on, or at least as near as possible to the main road through the village. Garnant then, like most of the villages in the mining valleys of South Wales, is like a length of string thrown carelessly on the ground – a skinny, scrawny, long drawn-out affair with no centre, roughly following the course of the river.

The main road runs along the lower slope of the southern side of the valley, so most of the houses sit above the river and the railway line which runs parallel to it, since both of those lie on the valley floor. Most of the houses on the side of the road further away from the river are a little higher than, and look down on, the houses on the opposite side of the road. In places where the slope is steep, the houses on the lower side of the road are shored up, or have been built with basements, so that they seem to be standing on tiptoe in a not-quite-successful effort to look the houses opposite in the eye. Apart from that there is no rhyme or reason to the shape of the village. Its houses have been built higgledy-piggledy, and its

37

few significant buildings slotted in separately here and there without plan or sensitivity.

Once the railway station which gave it its name had been built, the village had grown at a steadily accelerating pace, roughly up and down the valley from the spot where the short but steep road which climbs from the station joins the main road. That meant steadily closing the space between it and Glanamman, the next village down the valley, where the same process was going on, so that eventually the two villages met. Exactly where one ended and the other began seemed not to matter too much to anyone any more, except to postmen and various administrative bodies. In some ways the lives of the two villages were intertwined anyway. People from Garnant used Glanamman's small cottage hospital, some children from Glanamman attended the New School at Garnant because they lived much closer to it than to the school at Glanamman, the Baptist minister of Glanamman lived in Garnant, the rugby team whose playing field was in Garnant included players from both villages and was therefore called Amman United, and so on. But just as Pontamman, the community further down the valley than Glanamman, remained a little out of Glanamman's

The village of Garnant, in Cwm Aman

reach, so too did Gwaun-Cae-Gurwen, a smaller village further up but a little to one side of the valley itself, remain a little out of Garnant's reach, expansion in that direction prevented by a long, steep, winding hill with a steep cliff on one side and a gully on the other. Psychologically then, if you lived in Garnant, going down to Glanamman was a stroll, whereas going up to Gwaun-Cae-Gurwen was a bus-ride.

For those who only passed through it, the village must have seemed conspicuously undistinguished, a place one had to pass through to get to somewhere else, but itself a non-place, Nothingsville, with one way in and one way out. Gerard Manley Hopkins' 'Pied Beauty' ('Glory Be To God For Dappled Things') could never have been a theme poem in the social life of Garnant, or any village in the Amman or any other of the Valleys, for the people of the Valleys thought of life in black-and-white terms. They did that simply because their lives were lived in black-and-white terms. They were lived in black-and-white terms morally, and there was little slack. There were good men and bad men. A good man didn't swear, touch alcohol, read a Sunday newspaper, keep pigeons, race greyhounds, back horses, bet on card games, wear a scarf instead of a tie, go out unshaven, or do any manual work on Sunday. He went to chapel every Sunday with his family, shaved each day whether he intended to go out or not, gave his wife his wage packet unopened every Friday night, did the odd jobs around the house, and wanted his children to have a better life than he had. A bad man was the opposite.

Women too were either good women or bad women. In addition to doing daily chores such as preparing meals, making beds, cleaning the house and raising the children, a good woman washed clothes on Monday morning, hung them on the line in the garden in the afternoon, ironed them on Tuesday, patched and darned them on Wednesday, shopped on Thursday, baked bread and cakes on Friday, prepared the whole Sunday dinner except for cooking it on Saturday morning, paid her bills on time, went to chapel with her family – on Sunday evening at least (cooking the Sunday dinner was allowed as an excuse for not attending morning service) – wore a hat outside the house, didn't gossip, smoke, go to a pub, touch strong drink or ever swear. A bad woman was the opposite. The first time my mother bought a loaf of bread, I, the lowest in the family pecking order and presumably therefore the least likely to understand the import of what I was doing, was the one she sent to buy it, and I was instructed very clearly by her, several times, to tell the grocer to wrap it up well – a good woman just didn't run out of bread, of all things!

Life in the Valleys was culturally black and white too. Llewelyn ap Gruffydd, the last native Welshman to be a Prince of Wales, was killed by a soldier of Edward I of England in 1282, and after that the Welsh nobility decreased in numbers and declined in power and influence. Helped along by such strategies as the founding in 1571 of Jesus College, Oxford by Queen Elizabeth I, specifically for, among others, 'the sons of the Welsh nobility', most of the ruling classes were steadily anglicised also. In the end the Welsh were left a peasant people with a smattering of Welsh gentlefolk, a trickle of Oxbridge graduates who had not been thoroughly anglicised, and 'the Church' to offer cultural leadership and patronage, until the University of Wales was founded in 1872 and a new Welsh elite based on education emerged. Neither was there even one city in all of Wales until the 20th century, so that urban arts were absent from Welsh life until quite recently. Wales had no tradition of theatre, opera, orchestra, ballet or art galleries. Cultural activities were uniform: they were what you could do on your own in a village (such as write poetry), or they were what amateurs could do together in large villages and small towns (such as sing in choirs). There was for a long time too a religious black and white perception of truth that was inimical to many forms of art. 'Is a novel true?' 'Well, in a way, no.' 'Then it must be a lie.' The first real Welsh-language novel, *Rhys Lewis* by Daniel Owen, got by partly because it was subtitled, not too subtly, 'The Autobiography of a Minister'!

By the time I was born, a greater cultural diversity had begun. Amateur drama companies were springing up here and there, though the fare they offered was mostly sentimental, domestic and didactic. As the modern world slowly encroached, amateur opera companies were formed too. But the dominating religious environment, the rough-and-ready social environment, and the harsh economic environment still almost completely blocked out many of the lovelier things of life. There was little room for much refinement of taste in food, dress, manners or furnishing. The same was true of architecture. In time, the plain frontages of the box-like large chapels which had been spawned in the Valleys to meet the needs of fast-growing populations, often replacing the small, honest plain chapels with their simple functional beauty, were in many places overlaid by astoundingly pretentious and ugly facades. Artistically, for me as a child, there were words – Welsh-language poetry above all, and there was music, which meant choral singing. As regards other forms of art, my contemporaries and I were culturally deprived. Yet the Garnant of my childhood had at least many of the components which make a village a real fleshed-out village. It had, to begin with, its own distinctive characters.

There was Georgie Pike. Georgie was an Englishman. Not a Welshman who couldn't or wouldn't speak Welsh, but a man born and raised in England, and whose English accent had to be genuine, since it wasn't one anyone would want to emulate! How and why he ended up living in Wales, and Garnant in particular, I have no idea. He owned a horse and a four-wheeled open cart and went around the village selling fruit and vegetables, letting all the housewives know at the top of his voice that he was about and what speciality he had on his cart that day. He had a quick and ready wit, which was sometimes mildly ambiguous – 'I can let you have a lovely pea today' – and then came as close to being risqué as possible without some of his more proper women customers getting offended. Who knows, perhaps some of them even giggled once he and his cart had turned the corner.

Georgie had several black marks against him in addition to being 'a foreigner'. To begin with, he was that rarity in the community: a man who lived alone. Our local bachelors continued to live with their parents, and when those died were almost invariably either cared for by an unmarried sister who had also never left home, or were taken in by some married sister. Georgie also lived a little outside the village, and on the wrong side of the tracks, along a back road in a neat grassy clearing now completely overgrown. On top of that, his home, alongside which he kept his cart and behind which there was always a great pile of empty cardboard and wooden fruit boxes, was a one-storey structure made of wood – the only local habitation made of wood. Wooden houses were definitely not the norm in the Valleys, or the rest of Wales for that matter, and notwithstanding the fact that lots of the houses in the village were hardly going to win any prizes for architecture, there was a general feeling that a wooden house lowered the tone of the community! Even though perhaps no-one had ever been up close to, let alone inside Georgie's house, to villagers (most of whose houses were made from everlasting stone quarried locally), Georgie's house was a glorified hut, likely to fall down any minute or at least progressively to decay, and not too slowly. Just as well then that it was sequestered not only a good distance from the main road, but almost out of sight even from the back road on which it did stand.

Georgie was connected in some way to one other English family in the village that also kept a fruit shop, but very little else seemed to be known about his personal life. He wasn't disliked at all, or even disrespected; yet in our staid village, where even the oddities were our own and were defiantly claimed by us, Georgie was the most alien figure we had. This made him, for those who used scare tactics to discipline a child, a prime candidate for the role of bogeyman. Should children misbehave, they might well be told by some adult that Georgie Pike would come and take them away on his cart if they kept on misbehaving. As a result, when I was a boy I once failed to pluck up the courage to walk alone along the lane which for ten yards or so could be seen from Georgie's house, preferring instead to turn around, go back, and walk home by another and much longer route. In later years I discovered that Georgie was a kind and generous man, but he was enough beyond the pale to be caricatured and even demonised by some adults.

It would be a gross understatement to say that our village had a policeman. Not only did it have a policeman, it had a Gilbert and Sullivan policeman, as full-blooded and grand and gargantuan a policeman as ever walked a beat. He had a military moustache as wide as his face, which was so unerringly horizontal that it must have been waxed with the aid of a spirit level. If I were compelled to hazard a guess as to what he had been before he became a policeman, it would be that he had been a sergeant major in the British Army. He lived in the police station on the main road, and the mere sight of him standing at his gate, thumbs stuck into his uniform jacket just under the shoulders, watching passers-by and nodding unsmilingly and wordlessly at them, or walking along the road wearing his peaked cap, his silver metal buttons shining and with his short cape draped over his broad shoulders, was in itself a more than adequate peace-keeping force as far as little boys were concerned. Most of us also knew that – like all other authority figures in the community – the village policeman had the full moral support of our parents.

Unencumbered with the minutiae of endless trivial traffic offences, a village policeman in those days was free to devote his attention to such signs of potential real criminality as small boys spitting, swearing, playing cards, smoking, throwing fireworks through letter boxes and saying boo to old women. Our policeman was for me, at an impressionable age, such a formidable figure that I still stutter badly when a policeman speaks to me through the window of my car for any reason, and my wife has often had to smile charmingly, lean across, offer some explanation for my confusion other than strong drink or drugs, then carry on a chatty conversation with the policeman as if I didn't exist at all. Our policeman was known as PC Kay, and years went by before I discovered – when I moved to another village – that peeseekay wasn't one word which meant policeman!

The village had a barber shop, owned and run by Mr Cornelius, known affectionately – but behind his back! – as Corny (the other connotation of which hadn't yet reached Garnant). Corny was a courteous, slim, lithe, fair-haired, bespectacled and generously-moustached Englishman, of medium height and with a refined face. For some reason or other he too came to live in our village, and began to learn Welsh. Unfortunately, one day he was fooled by a couple of local smart alecs into believing some obscene Welsh words had respectable meanings. He used them in the wrong company, found out what had been done to him, never mentioned the matter to anyone apparently, but never tried a word of Welsh after that. Even after many years, some still remembered this incident, and feeling therefore ashamed of their community because of it, were always extra-respectful of Mr Cornelius. My parents would never fail to tell me very pointedly whenever I went to get my hair cut to 'be sure to be very polite to Mr Cornelius', as if, unable to tell him directly, they wanted him to know through their child's behaviour how they felt about what had happened, and that they were 'on his side'.

Corny's was the only place in the village I can think of where most of the village's male population went some time or other on a fairly regular basis, and Corny's charm (not a quality high on the list of requisite male traits in a mining community), his general knowledge, and the breadth of his interests, ensured that his establishment was a good place for worthwhile conversation. Unless the shop were crowded to overflowing, men would sometimes sit down again after they'd had a haircut and stay a while, just to continue to take part in some ongoing discussion.

Across the top of the seat in which his adult customers sat to have their hair cut, Corny would place a small plank on which little boys could sit. Until a boy reached a certain age, for some reason it would usually be his mother that would take him to have his hair cut. That could be not only embarrassing if there were a boy there younger than you and without his mother; it could lead to taunts of 'mammy's boy', and 'cissy' – nicknames that not only hurt badly at the time but that could easily stick and last. Sitting as far away from her as one could get away with and pretending you didn't know your own mother was personally satisfying, but worked only up to a point. Of the many rites of passage for a boy on the way to manhood – the first long trousers, the first cigarette, the first shave – the very first rite of passage in my village, the first of all those firsts and so the most satisfying by far, was to be allowed to go for the first time to Corny's, money in hand and unaccompanied by your mother!

Then there was Twm Check, a large, wide, pear-shaped and moon-faced man with straight black, thinning, gleaming, oily hair brushed back flat on his head in what was then known locally – and all over the civilised world we thought – as a backslash. He looked like a wheeler-dealer from American Prohibition days, or the mayor of a mountain village in Italy. He was certainly the closest we had to a mayor of our village, and he looked the part. He was, in fact, the generally genial host and manager of the local cinema. I say generally, because I encountered him only as a man one of whose professional challenges was to keep unaccompanied small boys in the front rows of the cinema quiet and in their seats.

I have always assumed that he gained his nickname from the loud checked suits that he often wore, but now that I think about it, it could be that his father had been what was called a 'check-weigher', a man at the colliery pithead who assessed the amount of coal sent up in drams from below by miners. I can't recall after all these years whether Twm Check smoked or not. If he didn't, he should have – but only the largest Havana cigars. Large Havana cigars were made for people who looked like Twm Check, and whether he smoked or not, it's much

45

easier for me to think of him as forever having a large Havana cigar in his mouth.

The village had its own institutions too. We had our own colliery, of course. It was around a colliery that most Valleys villages had originated. There had been other collieries in our village, but they had closed down by the time I was born. We were fortunate that the one colliery we had was still operating, since it had much to do with our self-esteem. You could hardly be a real, self-respecting village in a mining valley without your own colliery. It was bad enough that we had only one, when the next village up the road, Gwaun-Cae-Gurwen, to us a mere cluster of houses gathered around a railway crossing, had three.

Ours was called the Raven Colliery, and yet another assumption I had always made until a short while ago was that it had been named after the birds which congregated and nested in a grove of tall trees adjacent to the colliery, and whose unpleasant, harsh cries could be heard incessantly by all who passed by on the main road. I also assumed that the nearby Raven Inn was named after the colliery. But I have now been told on the very best authority that ravens don't congregate or nest in trees, and that the birds in those trees must have been rooks. For some time after that I thought that perhaps whoever named the colliery didn't know that, and so had made the same mistake as I had made. Now I know that the colliery was named after The Raven Inn. At someone's suggestion I visited the Inn one day and saw for myself hanging on a wall there a framed bilingual statement done in calligraphy, explaining that the Inn had long before adopted on its sign the three ravens which appeared as far back as the fourteenth century on the coat of arms of a local nobleman, Lord Dynevor of Dynevor Castle in a vale not far away, and in whose domain our village stood.

We had a rugby team, Amman United, made up of players from our neighbouring village, Glanamman, as well as from our village, but inasmuch as the ground on which the team played its home matches was in Garnant, we could and did claim it for our own when that suited us! Rugby was, of course, by far the prevailing sport in the Valleys. Until recently, rugby in Wales was an amateur sport, officially at least. In the past some local players, after becoming internationals, had gone to play 'up North' (the north of England, professional rugby country), and brought some sporting fame to the little-known Amman Valley by becoming household names there.

Amman United, like most local rugby teams, won a cup some year or other which gave the club a reputation that stood it and both villages in good stead for a long time. Mam's younger brother played for the team in its heyday. Tad-cu, who had no interest in rugby, was persuaded one day by his two other sons that as a father he owed it to his younger son to come and watch him play at least once. One Saturday afternoon he went. It was a game in which my uncle was marked by an allegedly (the allegers being his brothers) sly wing three-quarter, who kept tugging at his jersey when he didn't have the ball and when the referee was looking the other way (or so family tradition has it). My uncle finally lost his temper and spreadeagled his opponent with a punch to his jaw, right in front of the referee at one of those rare moments when the referee, unfortunately, was also actually looking at them! My uncle was consequently sent off the field, and Tad-cu was so ashamed that a son of his had been unable to control his temper in public, in what was after all only a game played with a few pieces of leather sewn together and filled with wind, that he never went to see a game of rugby again.

We also had an Italian shop. Every village and town worth its salt in the Valleys of South Wales had its Italian shop, its Carpanini's or Cresci's or Perego's or Bracchi's or Segadelli's, where hot and cold drinks and light meals – egg on toast, beans on toast, sandwiches and hot pies – were served, and confectionery, cigarettes and above all ice cream, was sold.

Our shop was Dalavalle's, and its proprietor Frank Dalavalle made a creamy, yellowish ice cream – the most wonderful ice cream I have ever tasted. He made it from the milk of two goats that he kept tethered on a grassy bank behind his shop, and I have always believed that the secret of his ice cream lay in those goats. Frank's three children, his two sons and his daughter, later took up the ice cream business, though they eventually turned to selling wholesale, winning awards along the way for quality, as they continue to do.

Frank started his business in 1917. Today there are Chinese takeaways and Indian restaurants galore in the Valleys of South Wales, but the Italian shops are still there too, their owners our senior immigrant families. By this time the Italians in South Wales have long been assimilated. Many of them speak Welsh fluently, and the names of their grandsons and great-grandsons appear on the books of local rugby teams. One of the children in my grand-daughter's class in her Welsh-medium primary school was Francesca Dalavalle, Frank's great-granddaughter!

Going into Frank's shop was a mysterious and awesome adventure for a child. There was, to begin with, and most conspicuously, the huge dragon of a coffee machine, which dominated the whole shop. And lest anyone be so abysmally short-sighted or so unbelievably preoccupied or so incredibly insensitive as to fail to observe and be suitably impressed with its sheer, dazzling, silvery presence, it made its presence known by issuing sounds as well. Now and then it simply burped gently, like a baby bringing up wind; other times it moaned and groaned and gurgled in low key as if it had eaten a meal last night it still hadn't been able to digest; but sometimes it hissed and spat steam so angrily and so *fortissimo* that it seemed not unreasonable to assume its god, perhaps an old Roman one, was furious with us all for something we had done, and was about to blow itself, and all of us with it, either to smithereens or to kingdom come. I have never been a mechanically-minded person, but some items of technology I have always wanted to try once – the public address system in a supermarket, the siren of a police car – and when I was a small boy I dreamed of being allowed one day to do whatever the things were that Frank Dalavalle did with his coffee machine.

Another thing which made a visit to Frank's shop a great adventure for a child were Frank's running quarrels with his family. Frank was forever yelling at his wife in the back room, whom he called Missus, or at his youngest child, his daughter Theresa, who was always under his feet somewhere, or at Joe and Bruno his two sons, wherever they might be. His gruff, unsmiling but friendly attendance in broken English on a customer was punctuated by these yells, which could be disconcerting not only because of their suddenness and volume and their seeming unrelatedness to anything Missus or Theresa or Joe or Bruno might be doing, but also because he yelled in Italian, the only completely foreign language I had up to that time heard of, let alone heard. As even an idiot could tell just by listening to Frank yell at his family, Italian was much more complicated than either Welsh or English. But what seemed like family quarrels was just a *modus vivendi*, for they were a close-knit family.

We had several pubs. Some were small converted dwellings with such delightful and question-begging names as The Lamb and Flag, The Prince Albert, and The Globe, names which rolled off the tongue like lyrical poetry. There was also the more prosaic-sounding and intelligible Colliers' Arms. The proprietors of those establishments were private individuals, who could therefore sell any beer they wanted to, and they proclaimed that fact with the words Free House on their signs – a confusing message for a small boy! But the flagship inns were The Raven Inn, halfway through the village, and The Half Moon (another lyrical touch) at the bottom end of the village, almost in Glanamman. These were purpose-built inns, owned by a brewery, and so only beer brewed by that brewery was sold there. They were much larger than the small pubs, and became centres for activities other than drinking and conviviality. Miners' Union meetings would be held in The Raven, and Amman United rugby team and whoever were their opponents for the day when they played at home changed and showered in an upstairs area at the back of The Half Moon. In some valleys the largest inns were owned by the owner of the local colliery, who sometimes also owned the brewery which supplied those inns with beer, and so much of the pay handed out to workmen on a Friday afternoon would be recouped on a Friday night.

A significant place in the village was the Reading Room, a room on the ground floor of a comparatively small building which had a billiard table upstairs. It contained a number of chairs around a very large table on which was spread out an array of newspapers and magazines, Welsh and English, local and national. Men who worked on the afternoon shift, with nowhere else to go of a morning perhaps, to avoid being under the feet of their wives while those were doing some household chores, could go along and browse in the Reading Room. So, of course, could men who were retired, or off work, either permanently because of some incapacity, or temporarily for some reason, perhaps a lay-off. How serious and avid was the reading that went on there could best be measured perhaps by both the volume of the 'sssh', and the intensity of the glare directed by readers there at anyone who broke the silence by saying anything more than a muffled 'good morning'. For a small boy, even to pop his head around the door to see if his father were there was a scary experience.

Twice a year, in early spring and late autumn, a funfair visited our village. The fair people would arrive in their gaily-coloured caravans first thing on a Thursday morning, coming from we-knew-not-where, and they would set up shop on a piece of wasteland which had become known as The Fairfield. Such fairs had originated ages before the valley had become industrialised, as places where farmers and smallholders came to trade. Some remnant of the trading aspect still remained when I was a child, with a few outside traders setting up stalls at which they sold china and cloths, but by then the fair was primarily a place for entertainment, with bumper cars, whirligigs, coconut shies, merry-go-rounds, gondola swings, and roll-a-pennys. For the time that they were there we children would pester our parents for extra pocket money, and our uncles and aunts for special donations. For three lit-up, music-filled nights, the fair people would ply their trade chirpily, then by the time people went to chapel on Sunday morning, they were all gone to we-knew-not-where, the fairground was empty and silent again, and nothing remained but forlorn scraps of coloured paper blown around by the wind on The Fairfield and memories of sounds and lights that had filled the night air.

There were local social events which we boys regarded as laid on primarily for our benefit. Weddings were a big deal for us, and we had scouts among us, the sons of mothers for whom details of such events were the stuff of life, who kept the rest of us well-informed about upcoming weddings – the day, the time, where the groom lived, and the route he and the best man would probably take to the chapel. It was traditional not only for the bride and her father but for the groom and his best man also to go to the chapel in a special, hired limousine, and by the time the day for the next wedding arrived we would have acquired a rope, and at the appropriate moment we would lie in wait at some strategic spot, a corner sometimes, where that limo had to slow down, or the middle of a straight stretch of road so that the driver would have plenty of time to see us. We would lay the rope on the floor across the road, then with some boys on one side of the road and some on the other, when the limo came into sight we would raise it and hold it up until the best man wound down the window on his side of the limo. A best man knew in those days that a best man had to do what a best man had to do if he were to get himself and his charge to the chapel on time and without any social opprobrium! And what he had to do was to have lots of coins in his pocket ready for such a moment, and to throw them out of the window when the limo was halted by a group of boys with a rope.

He wouldn't throw all his coins out of the window the first time he was stopped, for he knew there would probably be other boys with other ropes across the road further on, but once he had thrown some coins, usually a mixture of both copper and silver coins, we would drop the rope and allow the limo to move on while we scrambled on the road on our hands and knees. By this time, other boys who had played no part in the planning of the project would probably have gathered around and joined in, and so all thoughts of camaraderie were thrown to the four winds. We would compete furiously for the coins, shouldering someone else aside without looking to see who it was, putting a foot on one coin (and perhaps on a smaller boy's hand) while we picked up another coin. Then when the excitement was over we would all, friend and foe alike, compare our shares of the booty. The only problem was that there was no hard-and-fast rule about which side of the limo the best man sat – perhaps they didn't all read the same wedding-etiquette books – which could more or less upset your financial plans, certainly for that week, if you guessed wrongly, but generally speaking, the whole operation was quite literally money for old rope.

We would stop the car fairly close to the groom's home, since if we could collect the money and get organised quickly enough, it was fair game to try and get ahead of the car again and stop it once more. But that was only theory, I can't remember ever stopping a car twice. We would proceed to the chapel in any case, and stand together outside, because the best man, when he emerged from the chapel after the wedding service, would look around for us, and whatever coins he still had in his pocket he would fling toward us in one final, reckless act of abandon; one last extravagant, ostentatious gesture.

As a local social event for the general public however, a wedding was nothing compared to a funeral. A wedding was ultimately the result of a process of private decision-making. In size and ambience it became more or less what a bride and her parents decided for themselves they wanted and could afford it to be. But whatever decisions they made, there would be only two or three ministers at most at a wedding, and others who attended and participated fully in the whole day's proceedings were a limited number of invited guests. People who weren't guests, mostly women and children who were neighbours, could gather on the road the other side of the bride's home to catch a first glimpse of her as she emerged with her father to enter their limo. They could also go to the chapel and watch the proceedings there, and many did that too, but whereas the invited guests would sit downstairs, they would probably sit upstairs, and their attire would be far removed from the finery worn by the guests on that day.

But funerals were very special and grand occasions in the village then. Psychologically, socially and ritually the whole community seemed much more comfortable, and more competent, at dealing with sadness than with joy. Apart from women who gathered in the house of the deceased, and women who watched outside but might not attend the service in the chapel, a funeral was predominantly a male affair, although the males would be aware of themselves as representatives of their whole families. Even with that caveat, a funeral's size and ambience would reflect the instinctive response of the community at large to that particular death.

Most chapels had their own ministers, and ministers were social as well as religious leaders, so the depth of ministerial attendance at any happening added to the public estimate of that happening's significance and worthiness. A funeral could well be attended not only by a minister from every chapel in the village, but also by ministers from chapels in neighbouring villages. Every minister who attended a funeral would be given a part in the proceedings – in the service at the house of the deceased, in the gathering outside the house, in the service in the chapel, or in the service at the graveside. It might be a reading or a prayer or just the announcement of a hymn or the pronouncing of a benediction, but it belonged to the ritual that every minister did something, no matter how small.

A minister would be regarded as representing his chapel as well as himself, and so his presence at the funeral of a relative of a member of his congregation affirmed that member's standing in his or her chapel. But the community understood a minister's presence to say something about the minister too. A minister who didn't attend a funeral which was attended by every other minister in the village, perhaps even by a minister from his own denomination from a neighbouring village, would find life somewhat easier if he had a very good and public reason for not attending – like a broken leg! Conversely, the more funerals a minister attended, the more prestige he might gain locally, and it could compensate for his own professional limitations. So it might be said, 'Mr Williams isn't a very good preacher or scholar, but give him his due – he never misses a funeral!' It could add to his chapel's prestige also, for a minister's presence at a funeral might be reported approvingly in terms of the chapel he served, as in: 'The minister of Siloam was there!' And sometimes, when the name of the chapel was heavily emphasised, it had more to do with inter-chapel rivalry than with the simple imparting of information. What was being said was that the minister of some other chapel who in the view of the speaker should have been there, wasn't there, which didn't say much for that chapel!

No invitation was needed to attend a funeral of course, and most were well attended, since to begin with, the nuclear family was large then, the extended family was recognised, and there was a great deal of intermarriage between families. But attendance at a funeral was an investment too, since a family not regularly represented at funerals gained a reputation for that, which affected the number of people attending its own funerals, and how many attended one of its funerals was as good a public statement as any of the respect in which a family was held in the community.

Funerals were usually held in the afternoon, about an hour and a half after the day shift had ended in the collieries in the area, so that the miners (most of the men in the village) had time to hurry home, wash and change, take a quick bite, and then come to the funeral. If it were the funeral of a miner, particularly if he had still been working, there would be very many men at the funeral. If he had been killed in an accident at work, there would be very, very many men present.

A funeral would begin with a service in the home of the deceased, at which immediate family members, close friends and neighbours, and most of the ministers attending the funeral would be present. When that service was done, the first to emerge from the house would be the ministers. Men would already have gathered outside, someone would have distributed specially-printed hymn sheets among them, and the men would move forward toward the ministers. One of these would announce the first hymn on the hymn sheet; the precentor of the chapel which had been attended by the deceased would pitch the hymn, and the men would sing. At first, they would perhaps sing quietly, and the first hymn would always be in a minor key anyway, but they would usually end with a magnificent crescendo, some singing the melody, others singing the tenor and bass parts. Then, typically, on foot to a service in the chapel.

Sometimes, on our way home from school, we boys would see a funeral gathering outside a house. We would doff our caps, stop some distance away, and watch. If we were a clutch of boys together, we might well bet a few cigarette cards or marbles on how many ministers would emerge from the house. Sometimes we would pass or be passed by a funeral procession on its way to the chapel. The coffin would be borne on four men's shoulders usually (six if the deceased were heavy), until the undertaker called 'Change!', when another squad would step forward to take the place of the previous one. How often he would call for a change depended on the weight of the deceased, and whether it were very hot, or raining. We boys would sometimes follow the procession some part of the way, taking bets now on whether or not the undertaker would call 'change' before they reached the next lamp-post.

The coffin would occasionally be carried in a motorised hearse, with the mourners too in cars, but those were always signs of comparative wealth. Once, when a man died who was very rich by local standards, a friend and I gawped as the coffin was borne away from his home in a glass-sided hearse drawn by a pair of jet-black horses with black plumes on their foreheads, a hearse the twin of the one driven by Yul Brynner and on which Steve McQueen rode shotgun in one of the opening scenes of the film *The Magnificent Seven*.

In those days it was safe for children to play on the road, and on summer evenings we did – boys would play cricket, soccer, marbles, top and whip, and girls would skip and play hopscotch or rounders. Should a car come along, someone would shout 'Car coming!', we would halt whatever it was that we were playing, saunter to the side of the road, then move back and restart it when the car had passed. Many of those games must have been played by children like us, and exactly as we played them, for centuries, but most of them have become things of the past now.

It was also safe to wander further afield. Now and then a few friends and I would go even as far as Glasgow Pond, where in summer older boys carried large pebbles away from the bed of the River Amman until there was a pool under the narrow road bridge there not only deep enough for older boys to swim in, but deep enough for one or two of the more courageous and skilful among them to dive into from the bridge above, while passers-by would stop and watch, holding their breath in fearful anticipation of broken skulls. But the only danger to us we were ever aware of when we wandered was that of being bullied by older boys who resented our presence on what they considered their patch, or who perhaps simply wanted to make a difference in this world.

Even if the woman of the house should be out, there always seemed to be someone at home in those days – an elderly person, an unemployed man, an unmarried daughter, a man on the afternoon shift, and there was always someone calling – a neighbour, some family member, an insurance agent, a tradesman. The milkman came by every morning on his horse-drawn float, poured fresh milk from his churn into a half-pint measure and poured that as many times as necessary into the jug the housewife held out to him. The oil man, also with a horse-drawn cart, brought paraffin for lamps, heaters or cooking stoves, but he also carried a choice of lino and coconut mats. The fishmonger – the precise inflection and intonation of whose loud cry of 'Fish Alive oo-oh!' I could reproduce right now – brought fresh fish in a basket he carried on one arm, and cockles and laver bread in a basket he carried on his other. The rag and bone man too, who had long since turned to collecting old iron and sharpening knives, scissors and lawnmowers, also had his distinctive (although indecipherable) call.

Vendors from outside the valley reminded us there was another world out there. Johnny Onions came all the way from Brittany, wearing a black beret and pushing a large, old-fashioned, upright bicycle with so many strings of onions hanging from the seat, the crossbar and the handlebars that the bicycle itself was practically invisible. Some vendors became quite proficient not only at understanding colloquial Welsh but also at speaking it. Breton was a Celtic language, a sister tongue of Welsh, and so Johnny Onions had a head start, but one of my mother's brothers, when a student at the University College in Swansea some 20 miles from Garnant, while walking one day with a fellow student on the road outside the college found himself behind a black man. With the childish humour which besets students from time to time, he dared his fellow student – in Welsh – to kick him in the pants, only to have the black man turn around and challenge the fellow student – in Welsh – to try it! Where he came from I don't know, but a black man often came to our village, going from house to house carrying two huge suitcases which, after he had knocked on a door and the woman of the house had opened it, he would lay on the floor and open to reveal his wares – small brushes, polishes, soaps, dishcloths, shoelaces, boxes of matches. I have an aunt who swears that this man wasn't black but in fact a Jewish man named Black. She, however, having a tin ear for a good story, can't possibly be trusted on a detail of that importance!

difference

Black or Jewish, it made no difference to us. Although at one time, poor whites in the American deep South looked down on blacks, and needed someone to look down on, the idea of us, Welsh working class people, looking down on anyone for any reason – unless, perhaps, for some moral inadequacy – would be strange to us. Perhaps it's because we ourselves weren't looked down upon on a day to day basis by any others close to us. Perhaps it's because we only met people other and different to us in ones and twos, so there were never enough of them around to affect our lives in ways which make people feel insecure. Perhaps it's because as a people we have come into contact with few other groups we might have practised looking down on – which partly explains why tramps knocking on doors were a feature of life in the valleys, and they knew the best places. My grandmother would never let a tramp go from her door without a cup of tea, some sandwiches, and a few pence. She would say that it would be bad luck to turn a tramp away empty handed, but in her case certainly, it went very much deeper than that.

Our village, like other villages at that time, was a good place in which to grow old. There was no need for retirement communities. Families were large and most young people stayed in the valley, sometimes living with their parents even after marriage, or at least living nearby – perhaps next door. There was very often also an unmarried daughter or two living at home, an obvious feature of life then, partly resulting from the dearth of eligible young men following the carnage of the First World War. Neighbours would also be very helpful. Many front doors opened straight out onto the street so that even the very elderly and infirm who couldn't walk (or not very far), if they could be got up and dressed, on a fine day might be placed on an upright chair outside the front door. There they could watch the world go by and greet and be greeted by people walking past who might never come into the house for a visit, but were happy to stop for a brief chat on their way. For those confined to bed, their bed might be brought downstairs to a corner of the living room, so they could still be a part of the goings-on inside the house, hearing and contributing to conversations. And since old age was not at that point regarded as a communicable disease, nor equated with being completely out of touch with everything, old people weren't regarded as pariahs and could be useful, helping out with small chores such as shelling peas, darning socks, cleaning silver. Some could be listeners too, advisors even, to the young – and the not so young.

In many ways it was also a good time and place in which to be a child. Childhood had been, in terms of sickness and disease, a dangerous period of life for the generations which preceded mine, as the cemeteries of that time make abundantly clear. Fortunately, by the time I was born, a vast improvement was taking place in such matters, with school health visitors, community health workers, and children's clinics, and the beginning of family planning.

Children's behaviour was monitored, and their mischief kept within bounds, by the vigilance of the community at large. If people who knew your parents saw you keeping bad company, hanging around some area of danger or looking as if you were up to no good, they would take it upon themselves to warn you, or perhaps drop a hint to your parents, and with the exception of an interfering busybody or two, your parents would be grateful to them. Although a child might resent some particular interferences in his or her life, ultimately no child could escape the knowledge – even if they might resent that too, and fight against it – that in a deep sense, its immediate community was not an enemy but a society which cared for its own, especially the most vulnerable.

Neither were the young then so totally dependent on their peer group and the current scene for knowledge of life. A child could not but be aware of the wisdom distilled from universal human experience that was constantly bandied about by adults around them, in both casual sayings and formal proverbs. Some were put-downs to keep the young in

59

their proper place – 'the calf has nothing to teach the cow.' Some were behaviour-control sayings, although they might be at least half-believed by the adults, who had been brought up on them themselves – such as 'children should be seen and not heard' or 'eating fish makes you brainy'. But others were real, useful perennial truths put into words which burrowed into the mind and gave some shape and structure to life: 'Steady blows will break the stone', 'It's not good if you can do better', 'Keep your breath to cool your broth', etc, etc.

Not all things in the village that was my childhood world were as they should be, and that I knew. It wasn't uncommon on a Friday or a Saturday night to see a man stagger home to his wife and children, drunk as a lord. There were rough village characters such as Mrs Morris, who, though well past her prime, was still a big, strong woman, and one not to tangle with. On almost all except rainy days, she would sit outside her house, wearing a man's peaked cap, an apron made from old sacking, a woollen shawl over her shoulders, and watch the world go by. Passing Mrs Morris was a risk for a nicely-dressed woman on her way to chapel on a Sunday morning, or any other time for that matter, and passing by on the other side wasn't a solution since the road through the village wasn't that wide (and had no pavements). The decision was whether to acknowledge her or not, and either route could lead to abuse of the 'I suppose you think you're better than me because you're going to chapel' variety.

There were prejudices too. For a comparatively small village; we were astonishingly insular, within, for instance, our tight little denominational worlds. I cannot recall entering any chapel or church other than ours during my childhood, for any reason, and it was easy to regard people who were religiously different to us as odd. Indeed, other Christians might as well have been Hindus or Muslims. Nor was it only a matter of simple difference. We who were Congregationalists thought Baptists basic and cliquish, and as far as Calvinistic Methodists were concerned, they were so scarce in our valley that we simply wondered why they bothered to exist at all. Anglicans we regarded as stiff and dull, and Catholics as people who sinned outrageously all week, went to Mass and confessed on Sunday, and started the very same sinning all over again on Monday. It was a minor and irrelevant matter that none of us could identify a single Catholic except for our own local Italian family and perhaps an occasional cheerful, tough Irishman who had had little formal education, had no skills, had been forced to leave Ireland in search of work due to the primogeniture system, and had found work as a labourer for our Highway Authority, digging holes in our roads.

Yet, as far as I know, in practice such prejudices were as harmless as prejudices can be and still be prejudices. But then, perhaps we Congregationalists, being the largest denomination in the village, would be among the last to know about that, as we would be among the last to know what they all thought of us. And being the largest denomination in the village by far, we might not have let it trouble us either way.

Other aspects also of this world's imperfections entered into my young personal life. There were tragedies – Nanw, my mother's younger cousin; a strikingly lovely, auburn-haired girl, the only child of her parents, an apprentice hairdresser who gave me my first haircut; died when she was nineteen years old of tuberculosis, which we then called consumption. There were puzzles too – Mam-gu's younger twin sisters, Auntie Peggy and Auntie Annie, lived and worked in London. London was far away and another world to me. Yet they regularly came back to visit at Christmas time, loaded with gifts. Although they were only great-aunts to us, they would give my sister and me wonderful presents. I was very aware of Auntie Peggy and Auntie Annie, but why they should be living in London, and both of them, was something I wondered about for a long, long time, and whenever I asked I would be put off by being told everyone has to live somewhere, a reply which made the matter a darker mystery, of course. Only when I became an adult did I learn by chance one day that Auntie Peggy had discovered a knife under her husband's pillow one night, and that Auntie Annie's husband, Uncle Gwilym, who would sometimes take me and his smooth-haired black and white terrier, Spot, for rides in his green three-wheeler car, took his own life in a mental hospital.

The oldest of Mam's brothers took me to see him there once. I suppose he was thinking that I, a child, could be a crutch of some kind for him – a diversion perhaps, in what I assume he considered was likely to be a very difficult visit. We descended three steps to enter a large bare room with light green painted walls, which had in it one plain cupboard painted dark green, and a bed on which Uncle Gwilym was lying. Mam's brother gave him a small parcel containing home-made cakes, and the next thing he was bundling me quickly out of the room, the parcel following us through the air. But nobody tried to explain to me then the nature of his illness, and even when he died later, at his own hand, no one told me how he died, or even that he had. Looked at in its entirety, however, it seems to me that the village was a safe, full and good place in which to have spent my earlier years.

CHAPTER 3

Three Homes

ONE MEASURE OF Mam and Dad's early married progress through life, and so of my early development too, was the moves they made as a young couple from one house to another.

Mam was in one sense an odd one out among her seven siblings. Although a bright and lively person, she was the only one among them who never worked outside the home for a wage. At one time she had wanted to take one of two traditional outlets at that time for a young girl who wanted to work: to be apprenticed to a seamstress locally, or to undergo training as a nurse outside her valley. But a touch of rheumatism she had suffered as a child had made Tad-cu extra-protective of her, and he had persuaded her to stay at home, using her mother's need of help as an excuse. With six other children in the family younger than her, this excuse might well in fact have also been a genuine reason. Either way, from the then school-leaving age of 13, stay at home is what she did, so when she married she had never had any income of her own to put any of it by.

When Dad left school, he went straight to work, first in a tinworks in the village in which he was born and raised, Glanamman, and later at several coal mines up and down the valley. It was an established custom in the Valleys in those days for an unmarried son living at home to give his mother his unopened wage packet each Friday, from which she would feed and clothe him and give him some pocket money. It was also an honourable tradition for the mother to put aside some part of the money he gave her and save it to give him on the day he got married, a start in his new life. In that respect, however, Dad's mother failed him: she didn't do that.

Life had been harsh for her. I remember her as an unemotional, very wrinkled, toothless old woman, her hair drawn back and tied in a bun, and with the kind of profile that Dylan Thomas once described as 'a fist of a face'. She showed no more interest in me than did Dad's father, but then my existence was hardly a new and exciting experience for her either, since one or two of her eight eventual grandchildren were teenagers by the time I was born.

She had given birth to and raised three girls and five boys, in the days when there weren't washing machines or vacuum cleaners or electric cookers, let alone nappies or sliced bread. I doubt that her husband had ever been much of a partner for her, as a spouse or a parent. He was a stocky, hunched, gruff, sullen man, always surrounded by a smell of acrid smoke coming from an ancient pipe that he never took out of his mouth, except, I assume, when he went to bed. Whenever we called to see them his first question to Mam was 'Have you brought me any tobacco?' There was a time when Mam would take him a tin of tobacco when she visited their home, but when that question became his opening greeting on every visit she made, it angered her, she told me, and she stopped taking him any tobacco at all – although that didn't stop him asking his question.

That must have been before I was old enough to pay any attention to such matters, since I don't think I ever saw his pipe full of fresh tobacco. All that it had any time I was there and noticed was just some old, half-smoked tobacco at the very bottom of the pipe's bowl – mixed, I suspect, with as much old ash as tobacco, since it was forever going out and he was forever having to relight it.

As he too was a coal miner, his wages also were subject to the operating profit of the mine, and so Mam-gu Glanamman, his wife, had supplemented his earnings when the children were small by practising as a midwife. She had no formal qualifications, but in those days there was no midwife of any other kind around. In wintertime she would often leave home carrying a small bag full of her necessities, walking up the hill behind the house or crossing the bridge to the other side of the River Amman to some farm up on the mountainside. She might stay there for as long as a week or two waiting for the farmer's wife's time to give birth, for should it snow heavily it could be very difficult for anyone to come down to the valley to get her when the birth was imminent, and it might be even more difficult for her to get up to the farm. Judging from wistful comments I heard Dad make from time to time over the years, whether from choice or necessity she was often absent from her home when her own children were small, as a result of calls for her services as a midwife.

Her firstborn, Jack, ran away from home and volunteered for the army in World War I before he was old enough to enlist. He was discharged and sent home but enlisted again as soon as he was 18. After the war, without coming home, and without corresponding with his parents or any of his siblings except (for some reason Dad himself never understood) Dad, he joined the Indian Army. He later went on to Australia, qualified there as a cattle inspector, joined the Australian Army in World War II, became a sergeant major, and finally made contact again with his mother and came home to visit her at the very end of her life. How capable she was of love I don't know, but I suspect that her firstborn's absence from so much of her life was a deep wound.

All Mam-gu Glanamman's other four sons became coal miners. In addition to them needing clothes bought, cleaned, washed, ironed and mended, they also needed their bedrooms cleaned, their beds made and changed, hot meals that were basic but large and nutritious prepared, and also bread and cheese or an apple, perhaps even a sandwich, a flask of tea and hopefully a piece of cake or fruit pie provided to take to work every morning of every working day. Every working day too they and her husband returned home from the colliery, coal dust covering their faces and hands, coal dust in their nostrils and ears and hair, coal dust impregnating their clothes. They wanted (and needed) first a hot bath, next clean clothes, and then a hot meal. As her daughters grew, they could help with the household chores, but eventually they, and two of her sons, got married and set up their own homes, whereas her other two sons remained bachelors and coal miners. Long after her husband had retired, those two sons continued to live at home and she continued to prepare food, clean, shop, wash, iron and mend for them, and (though the house had no inside plumbing) have a hot bath ready for them every working day almost till her own dying day.

But even those whom life victimises can victimise others. She had favourites among her children, and Dad wasn't one of them, something which affected him all of his life. He had brothers who called at a pub on the way home from work every Friday – pay day – opened their pay packets there, spent as much as they wanted to on beer, then returned home the worse for wear, and gave their mother what was left. Dad didn't drink, and every Friday took his pay packet home unopened to his mother, but the day he got married all she gave him was a meagre ten-shilling note. He never again slept overnight under that roof, and returned to his former home only for brief, formal visits. On those visits he would never, for instance, go into the pantry to see if there were something to eat there that he fancied, whereas that would be the first thing he would do when he visited his in-laws' house.

Life had been hard for Mam's parents too. They had also raised eight children, but for whatever reasons they, together, did a better job not only of resisting the downward pulls in their environment but of responding to the upward ones. Their wedding gift to Mam and Dad was to insist that they live with them in their home (despite there being six of Mam's siblings still living there) for one whole year, buying their own food but paying no rent and contributing nothing to heating, lighting or any other domestic bills during that time, so that they could save a little for their future. At the end of that year, with a two-month-old daughter, Mam and Dad moved to a ground floor flat in a two-storey house that was to be my first home, for it was there that I was delivered twelve months later, a 10 lb baby, with my own grandmother, Dad's mother, as the midwife.

The house containing the flat was one of a handful on a road called Jolly Road – named after an old inn there bearing that name, a fact remembered by no one now apart from a local historian or two. Jolly Road was close and parallel to the main road which ran through the village, but a fenced-in railway track ran between them. So vehicles going from Jolly Road to the main road had to take a long way round, though that was a matter only for delivery vans, coal-carts or visitors with cars. No one living in Jolly Road then owned a car, they all reached the main road directly by crossing a footbridge over the railway line.

Mam's three brothers, one just 20 and two in their late teens, crossed the footbridge to call on us one evening, for the sole purpose, apparently, of finalising a process they thought had gone on long enough – the choosing of a name for me.

Vivian Jones in Jolly Road today

Three names were put into a hat: Meirion, Eifion, and Vivian. The choice reflected something of the indeterminacy of the Welsh consciousness at that time. The first two are not strong-sounding, but do have a Welsh pedigree; while the latter, the name that came out of the hat, comes from the same Latin root as 'vivacious', and means 'lively'. It was a common enough name for a boy in my part of Wales then, which was probably partly to do with the fact that Vyvyan was the name of a well-known land-owning family in the area. Two other boys in the village were also called Vivian, and in the next village in which I lived there were four Vivians – two of them Vivian Jones!

I have never much liked it as a Christian name. It is neither Welsh nor unambiguously masculine, and apart from one West Indian cricketer, I know of no man of any import whose first name is Vivian. Dad apparently wasn't at home during this undignified process. But that he presumably acquiesced to the choice of name when he did come home, instead of insisting on cutting a better deal for me, is one of the very few grudges I hold against him. I wasn't even given a middle name to offer me a possible alternative should I ever feel the need for one. Of course, there was no way for anyone around my cot that night to foresee the trouble that name would bring me one day in the United States, where it was always, always, a woman's name – notwithstanding even the fact that John Wayne's real name was Marion! But in America it did at least occasionally give one some mileage conversationally, and Americans didn't easily forget a man called Vivian! It has crossed my mind too that were I inclined to attach significance to portents, Vivian and Jolly could be grist to that mill!

Before I was three, we moved to my second home in Garnant, the house I remember best there. It was one of a row of four small linked cottages, above and parallel to the main road, and just a little way from it. Cottages in this case didn't mean quaint, ivy-covered homes approached through a creaking garden gate and up a curved path perfumed with lavender and skirted by hollyhocks. These were crudely-built structures of local stone, their walls covered with a plaster freshly painted a yellowy-orange ochre colour every spring, fronting an unsurfaced lane along which they were approached from the road.

Our official address was 2, Upper Bank. I can only surmise that the word Upper was in reference to the main road below, since there was no Lower Bank. But the cottages were known locally as Chinatown. To this day I haven't been able to find out why they were called Chinatown, but on being asked where you lived it was easier to say Chinatown straight away, even though people laughed every time you said it. No one knew where Upper Bank was, so you would have to say Chinatown in the end anyway.

David Jones and his family lived in Number 1, we lived in Number 2, I have no recollection of who lived in Number 3, but Mrs Phillips lived in Number 4. Every child should have a David Jones as a next-door neighbour. He was a thickset, slow-moving, gentle, kind and thoughtful man. His wife gave birth at home to a daughter one day, and the next day he came into our house to fetch me and to take me by the hand to see the new baby. A week later, he once again came into our house to fetch me. The little child had died. David Jones took me by the hand into his cottage, this time to see the now still infant, dressed in a long white silk gown, lying in a small coffin bordered with lace. I have no doubt that, rather than concocting some story about her disappearance, and having surely first asked my parents whether he might do so, he wanted to introduce me gently to the physical reality of death. Although I can't now remember my feelings and thoughts at the time, I can recall David Jones talking quietly to me, explaining to me that she really wasn't with us any more now, and I can recall being invited by him to put my hand in his and let his hand guide my hand to touch that little, cold, smooth, precise, pale and lovely face. I did so, without fear, and I have no sense at all of any ill effects either then or later as a result of the experience. I feel sure that he did wisely and well. Many years later I read of psychologists in New York talking of beginning a new speciality called thanatology (*thanatos* being the Greek word for death). They did so as a result of the number of people they were having to treat who were suffering from being denied an encounter with the corporeal reality of death when they lost a loved one.

Mrs Phillips in Number 4 was a prominent feature of my audio experience at a tender age. She seemed forever to be outside the back door of her house yelling for her husband at the top of her voice, though I have no idea why on earth she wanted him so often, or where he might possibly have been when she called. I can remember Mrs Phillips' appearance well – a woman with a few grey strands in her jet-black hair, a thin, sallow face, high cheekbones and rimless glasses, but I have no recollection at all of her husband. For all I knew, he never, ever came when she called.

Mrs Phillips had two children, an older daughter with whom I had little to do, and one just a little older than me, a straight-haired, freckled, pleasant, adventurous, capable girl. She was also a tomboy. Proof of that was that she forever had scratches on her arms and legs, and often on her face too. Sometimes those were the result of scrambling through hawthorn hedges laced with brambles, but sometimes they were the result of being over-friendly to strange cats or dogs, for she passionately loved creatures of all kinds. She ranks high on my list of people who for a while were more than a footnote in my story, whom I have never seen since, but would like to meet again to see what they have made of life, and what life has made of them.

Our cottage was very small. First of all, it didn't have much headroom. One Christmas morning Mam's three brothers, all younger than her, returned from the 6 a.m. service held in Hen Bethel up on the mountainside, but instead of going back to their own home came to ours. Presumably they thought that the place to be on Christmas morning was somewhere where there were children, and Mam was the only one of their two married sisters who had children. They knocked on the front door, quietly so as not to disturb our neighbours. Mam recognised their voices as they muttered to each other. The cottage only had one bedroom, and I heard her tell Dad in a whisper to pretend he was asleep. Everything was silent for a few minutes, then on the one small window, which began almost at the floor level of the bedroom, there was a tapping sound. I looked across and saw a face peering through. One of them, helped by another, had managed to stand on the shoulders of the third, and short though they all were, that was enough to enable him to peer through the upstairs window!

Downstairs the house had only two rooms: a living room in the front, and behind that a room which we called the scullery, where Mam cooked and did the washing. Under the small, nine-paned living room window, and with its back to it, was a settle. Tight up against that was a wooden table with an unvarnished surface which Mam scrubbed every day, and at which we ate our meals or played games, or at which various chores such as shelling peas or making spills were carried out. Water came from a tap in the lane outside, which was shared by the four cottages. The water was carried into the house, drinking water in a metal pitcher, washing water in a bucket – and we washed in cold water in a bowl on a table in the scullery.

Our privy was outside, at the top of the garden behind the house. At that time, top-of-the-garden privies were a conspicuous feature of life in the Welsh Valleys. Some of them were primitive, minimal affairs not to be caught dead in for some people, and not for anyone to be caught in, dead or alive, in a high wind. They would be ramshackle, rickety structures, with wooden walls, an earth floor, no window, a zinc roof, and a shaky door with a loose catch. They were extremely draughty, and a prime place for catching pneumonia. Other outside privies were secure little palaces, with brick walls, a slate roof, a door with a proper handle, a lock with a key inside, a cement floor covered with lino over which there might be a rag mat, a window with curtains, even, perhaps, a vase of fresh flowers on the window sill each day. To see one of those would be to understand why the Welsh phrase for privy is *tŷ bach*, which means 'small house'.

A visit to a top-of-the-garden privy was a public affair in the sense that one went to it in full view of all the neighbours, and of passers-by if the house were close to a road. Yet ironically, in the days of large families and small houses, the privy, wherever it was situated, was in fact the only place where, once having entered it and closed the door, anyone could enjoy privacy without fear of interruption – and could refuse to be rushed. In an ethos in which privacy was at a premium, it was used by some as a retreat! It wasn't uncommon at all to see a neighbour walk up the garden path to his top-of-the-garden privy in the morning after breakfast, in slippers and wearing a cardigan, hair neatly combed, spectacles in one hand, newspaper in the other, and emerge only after a long time. It's the way things were. An uncle of mine moved to London and lived there in a comfortable house with an inside WC, but was never able to disabuse himself of the idea that that was the place to read the morning newspaper.

The floor of the living room in our cottage consisted of flagstones, covered here and there by loose rag mats Mam had made. There was no gas or electricity, and the living room would be lit at night by an oil lamp resting on the table. It had a brass base which supported a translucent, light green glass receptacle which contained the oil. That had an opening on top with a metal collar threaded on the inside, into which a metal double-wick casing was screwed, the lower ends of the wicks hanging down into the oil below. A clear glass funnel fitted on top of the casing. When night fell, the lamp would be brought out from a cupboard in the thick stone wall beside the fireplace, the funnel removed, the two wicks turned up low and lit, and the funnel replaced. The wicks were kept low until the funnel had begun to warm, and then they would be turned up. The lamp gave a surprisingly good light in the centre of the room, although of course corners were left in shadows and darkness. Sometimes at night-time Mam would carry the lamp in her hand to the scullery to fetch something, and unless dad were there also, my sister and I, frightened of the dark, would stop doing whatever we were doing and follow her, holding on tightly to her skirt.

The living room had a high, open coal fire, with horizontal iron bars in front. One night when Mam had gone to the cinema with a friend, Dad sat on a chair he had placed before the fire, and took both my sister and me onto his lap so that he could read to us from a well-known book in Britain at that time, Arthur Mee's *Children's Encyclopaedia*. Dad bought such books ostensibly to read to us, but I don't doubt that deep down he bought them to educate himself as much as to educate us. Resting on the fire was a zinc boiler, full of water being heated so that we two children could be given our weekly bath by Dad before going to bed – which meant it was a Friday night. Suddenly there was a crash, a loud hissing sound, and steam enveloped us. In a moment the air was full of fine ash. The fire had burned out inside, leaving only an outer shell of coal. Its top had collapsed inward, and the boiler had lurched sideways pouring water over the fire. Poor Dad had first to ensure we were out of harm's way, next take the boiler down from the fire, and only then do as much cleaning as he possibly could before Mam returned. I don't remember her return, but I haven't forgotten the name of the man Dad was reading about to us when that fire collapsed, although the next time I came across it I was in my fifties, living in the United States, and reading Alistair Cooke's *America*. The man was Amerigo Vespucci, who Cooke described as 'a Florentine businessman and promoter, who promoted himself so well that he got his name attached first to South America, and then to the whole continent, though he took no part in the early voyages.'

We had no radio, let alone television. Neither did my sister and I at first have much in the way of toys. But as often as he could, Dad would play games with us. The settle in the living room was so tight up against the table that we children, who weren't strong enough to shift the table, had to climb over the arms of the settle in order to get on to it (a handy cage for busy youngsters at meal times). My sister and I would sit on it, Dad

73

would sit on a chair the other side of the table, and we would play our simple games. 'Hide the button' was one. A button was all the equipment needed. Dad would take it first, place both his hands behind his back, return them to the table tightly closed, then one of us would guess in which hand the button lay. If that guess were wrong, Dad would hide his hands again, return them to the table, and the other would try. So it went on until one of us guessed correctly, and won the right to hide the button ourselves. A score was kept, each person earning a mark when another failed to guess in which hand he or she held the button. The greatest thing about this and similar games was that Dad was playing with us, and that, of course, wasn't only because children (and adults for that matter) need undisputed referees to be able to do anything competitive successfully. In time we acquired such games as Ludo, Snakes and Ladders, and Draughts, and with each acquisition our playtimes became a little more sophisticated.

We all slept in the same bedroom. I, the younger child, would go to bed first, candlestick in hand as I climbed up the stairs. I would put the candlestick down on the table at my bedside, and dive headfirst under the sheets for a few minutes, letting my head warm the cold spot where my feet would lie. Then I would emerge again to put my head on the pillow and watch the candle. Sometimes it would burn with a small, ordinary flame, sometimes it would reach upward as high as it could until it tapered off narrowly and sharply into black smoke, and at other times some draught would cause it to flicker wildly and throw frightening fast-moving shadows on the walls. After a while it would probably be Mam who would come upstairs to see if I were ready to go to sleep. She would make sure I had said the Welsh version of 'Now I lay me down to sleep', then she would bid me goodnight and go downstairs again, taking the candle with her. I would struggle hard to try and keep awake until my sister came up – peering into the gloom, straining my eyes to make things out – before the 'holy darkness' closed in on me. I would always be fast asleep before my sister arrived.

Our house was only a quarter of a mile away from Tad-cu's house, and the traffic between the two homes was two-way and regular. I would often be taken across to Tad-cu's house, and perhaps left there for hours on end. Apart from one visit by Tad-cu, I have no recollection of either him or Mam-gu visiting our house, but one or more of Mam's sisters and brothers were always turning up at our door, perhaps just for a change of scenery, perhaps to share a piece of good news or to talk over some problem, perhaps to avoid some chore at home, perhaps because of some temporary quarrel with a sibling, perhaps even, who knows, to see my sister and me. Having come, they would help my parents with this or that task – ironing, digging the garden, shopping, washing my sister and me, dressing us, taking us for a walk, preparing us for bed. Would that all children had as many caring family members living close by, and would that all young couples with small children had such a strong support system.

The most memorable event for my parents while they lived in Chinatown was that my sister, after walking home from school one wet day in shoes which (unknown to them) leaked, developed both double pneumonia and meningitis. Then it was that someone entered our lives for a comparatively brief period, never to be a part of our lives again except from a distance; but in that brief period, in the eyes of my parents, she achieved the status of sainthood.

The first District Nurse appointed to our village had just begun her work there when my sister became ill, and my sister would surely not have lived but for a quality of dedication from her that's rare, that could never be bought with money, and that no District Nurse could possibly give all even of her seriously-ill patients day after day, year in year out. But my sister was Nurse Jones' first seriously-ill patient and she was determined not to lose her.

I remember Nurse Jones in her later years, wearing her navy blue uniform, white collar and small, navy blue cap. She was a little hard of hearing by that time. A tall, handsome woman whose professional skills and dignified demeanour was an uplift for a whole community, she never married. I have come across many instances in valley life of women who for this, that and the other reason – the demands of work, their professional status, their strength and quality of character – seem to most men in a working-class community to be beyond their aspirations as a potential life partner. Yet such women often lead lives of such worth, and become such recognised pillars of the community, that it is presumptuous for any of us to assume that being single has been for them a simple negative, if a negative at all.

I was told little, and was too young to have understood more, about my sister's illness. I was taken to stay at Tad-cu's house as soon as she became ill so that I would not hear her screams at night, and so that my parents could give her all their attention in the time before she was taken to be operated on at the hospital in Swansea, the nearest large town (later given city status by Queen Elizabeth to mark her gift of the title 'Prince of Wales' to Charles, her firstborn, when he turned 21). I can remember being taken to Swansea by my parents one day when they went to visit her, but I was left outside with an aunt. It was a cold, bright, sunny afternoon. When my parents emerged again, I was standing with my aunt at the front gate of the hospital. I was told to look upward, and my gaze was directed to a small figure waving from a bed in a glass-fronted annexe on the first floor. I was told it was my sister and to wave to her, and I did.

The biggest thing that happened to me while I lived in Chinatown was that it was from there that I first went to school. It was the very day of my third birthday. I couldn't begin before I was three, and it wasn't required that I start that young, but I was lonely and bored at home. I wanted to go to school, the school had room for me, my sister was there already and Mam's sister taught there, which probably made Mam more at ease with an early start for me.

There were two primary schools in our village: the National

School, product of a long-established Anglican movement for children's education, and the school I attended, the New School. After a very honourable record, the National Schools have ceased to exist, but the New School was run by the local education authority and until a few years ago was still going strong, and still called the New School, but now it has been replaced by a brand new school.

The day I was three then, I walked almost a mile to the New School, mostly along the main road through the village. There were no pavements along the way, but neither were there many cars on the road, nor were those that were in evidence driven so quickly then as to be a great concern. My sister, however, had been instructed to hold one of my hands all the way, while in my other hand I carried a small oblong brown tin box in the shape of a tiny travel case, only big enough to contain a few sandwiches and an apple to eat at lunchtime. A bottle of milk was provided by the school. It was the beginning of getting to know the world outside my family. It was also the beginning of years of attendance at educational institutions.

One bedroom only for two parents and two children, one of each sex, couldn't be an appropriate sleeping arrangement for long, and before I was four, we moved again. This time it was to a three-bedroom house, with gaslight – but only downstairs – and rented to my parents by Uncle Bob, Mam-gu's brother. As with most houses in the village, it had a name: Mountain View. The mountain in view from the front windows of the house when it was built was the Black Mountain on the northern side of the valley, but by the time we came to live in the house, the view of the mountain had been interrupted by a house on the other side of the road. Yet even if the name of the house didn't reflect the truth about the view any more, it represented another kind of view, held strongly at that time, especially among the leaders of Welsh society: the view that the Welsh language was well past its sell-by date, that that wasn't a big deal, and that English was now the language which conferred dignity, the language which should be used for all things formal. Chapels that used only Welsh on the inside would have English inscriptions on the outside, and local stores with aspirations would bear such names as London House, or Manchester House.

Mountain View was the middle one of three attached houses. It had a front door with a large window on the right side, and on the right side of the window a latched door leading into a covered corridor through which one gained access to the back of the house.

The move to Mountain View wasn't far in terms of distance. However, the fact that we moved a little further down the valley, to a house on the main road, and in the centre of the village, made a difference. Tad-cu's house, Jolly Road and Chinatown were all at the far eastern end of the village, and off the main road. The area that comprised Chinatown and Tad-cu's house was even something of an enclave, closely knit, almost everyone Welsh-speaking, with three shops between our house and Tad-cu's house – a sweet shop, a fish and chip shop, and a small grocery store in the front room of a house. But the house on one side of Mountain View had a lean-to shed attached to it in

Mountain View

78

which Maggie Jones, our elderly, kindly, short-sighted spinster neighbour on that side, kept a sweet shop.

On the other side was the village post office, and on the other side of the road the ironmonger's shop had one petrol pump in front of it. A hundred yards up the road was a furniture store, a bakery and a fish and chip shop. Another hundred yards and there was a Co-operative store, a newsagents, the Raven Colliery, The Raven Inn, and a large billiard hall. Another hundred yards or so again and there was a butcher's, another fish and chip shop, and a ladies' hairdresser. In the other direction, down the road, there was a grocery store, a road turning down toward the railway station, a chemist's, another hairdresser, and a bank. For the first time in my young life we also had a next-door neighbour, Mrs Roberts the postmistress, who spoke no Welsh. There were several whole families around us now who spoke no Welsh, and the children of some of those became friends of mine.

One part of my life was over. Born in a flat on the wrong side of the tracks, my first move had been to a cottage on the outskirts of the village. I had now moved close to the geographical centre of the village, and in doing so I had unwittingly taken a first, tiny step in the direction of today's urbanised, anglicised cosmopolitan world!

Mountain View was the last house in which I lived in that village. I am surprised at how little I remember about it – about its rooms, its furniture, how the furniture was arranged, its fireplace, its garden, even the bedrooms, including my own, although I remember that my bedroom overlooked the road. My memories of Mountain View are sporadic. I can recall waking up in the dark one Christmas morning and finding three gifts on my bed: a torch, a toy gun, and a Welsh-English New Testament; all symbolic, I once fancifully thought, of basic aspects of the grown-up world which awaited me. I can recall crying on another Christmas morning because one of Mam's brothers was looking over my new books, another was checking out my new jigsaws and games, while the third was putting my black, streamlined Hornby engine (with red coaches) and its rails together for me, and it was Christmas morning and I had nothing at all with which to play.

I can recall not responding immediately when Mam called me to her one day, only to discover when I finally went to her that what she had wanted was to give me a penny to go and buy myself a cornet from an ice cream van which had been passing the house when she called. I remember vowing that from that day onward I would always, no matter where I might be at that moment or whatever I might be doing, and no matter how inconvenient it might be for me, honour my mother by going to her immediately every time she should call me. I can also remember an ambulance coming suddenly one morning to take Mam away to hospital. Dad tried to reassure us that we needn't worry, that everything would be alright, that Mam would soon be back home with us again. He told us that all she needed was to have her appendix taken out, and he tried to explain what that meant, but it was still traumatic to see Mam taken away from us in a strange white vehicle, by strangers in white coats.

There is so much a child doesn't understand, so much that isn't explained, or not adequately, so much he or she has to take on trust. I can't, however, have been all that traumatised when Mam was taken to hospital, since what happened didn't seem to affect my appetite in the slightest. I can recall the disappointment I felt when I faced the first meal poor Dad had prepared for us, about an hour after Mam had gone – the midday meal. Just boiled garden peas on a plate, with bread and butter. As I loved him and respected him and would never want to hurt his feelings, I didn't say anything; but I can remember thinking that, despite short notice, a man of his age should surely have been able to provide us with richer fare than that, and I very much hoped he was going to get his act together and do much better at that chore as our motherless days wore on. But apart from such episodic memories, few other memories have remained. We must have had a garden, but what was it

re why Few memories of home @ Mt View — opp of how I am w) Morgun & house

like? Was it a large one? Did we have any blackcurrant bushes, or apple trees? Where was the privy? I have no idea at all of the answers to such questions.

I have wondered about the scarcity of my memories of Mountain View, especially compared to how much I can remember about our cottage in Chinatown. I'm sure it isn't because I was at all unhappy there. Perhaps it's just that in Chinatown I had been too young to go far afield, even after starting school, so it was at home, in the cottage itself or around the cottage, that I had spent most of my time. By the time I arrived in Mountain View I was a growing boy, eager to spend every spare moment in the company of other boys, imbibing from the more knowledgeable among my peers (usually boys with older brothers) important information such as the three ways of getting rid of warts or where one could find wild rhubarb suitable for making into peashooters, and learning new essential boy skills such as how to whittle a whistle from an ash branch or how to spout a mouthful of water in one continuous, well-directed stream through a gap in one's teeth, or being introduced, through playing marbles, into the male world of competition, of winning and losing, of the satisfaction of beating someone else or the ignominy of being beaten oneself. I was beginning to go out beyond the home, as far abroad as my friends and I dared, to explore the surrounds and the most distant corners of our village, to scour our whole wide world for tadpoles and sticklebacks and birds nests, to steal apples and pears from the gardens of foreigners in other lands who, even if they saw us as we ran away, could not possibly know who we were – although, as later encounters with irate fathers made clear to us, we did sometimes get that part wrong.

Increasingly too, as I grew older, male adults in the family would want to take me with them to various places. Sometimes I would be taken to a billiard hall care of Mam's three brothers, who would by this time be in their early twenties, and were all students. Billiard halls were very conspicuous features of Welsh

81

mining valleys in those days. They were bare, spartan places, with thick, dark brown lino floors, and wooden benches raised on platforms around the outer walls, which were painted light brown. They were clean, aseptic places too, bearing a strong smell of carbolic. They were also well-run places, with signs on the walls making it very explicit – in plain, bold black print – that spitting on the floor, bad language and betting were strictly prohibited!

Another uncle, Mam's older sister's husband – they had no children of their own – also liked to take me somewhere with him from time to time. He worked for the Great Western Railway, and once took me with him on a train to collect his weekly wages at a depot a few stations away. It was an expedition which came close to making this book impossible for me to write.

We travelled alone in a closed compartment. On both sides it had a very heavy window which formed the upper half of the door. To open a window you held a thick leather strap attached to the base of the window, pulled it hard toward you, waggled it up and down hopefully, and if something at the base of the window clicked, and didn't catch you unprepared, and if you weren't too weak to hold the strap as the window fought to crash its way downward, you struggled to control the strap by letting it slide through your hands slowly. It was difficult even for an adult to open one of those windows, but that day, after fiddling with it unsuccessfully on the outward journey, I eventually managed to open one on the return journey. It came down with a bang loud enough to make even an uncle as laid back as Uncle Tom raise his head for a second from the newspaper he was reading and say, 'Naughty boy! Now don't put your head out.'

Opening the door of a Great Western Railway carriage from the inside, however, was absolutely impossible even for most adults. It had a sliding catch which called for a blacksmith's fingers to make any impression on it. While that was an excellent safety feature (whether that was the purpose behind the design or not), it also meant that most people, as they arrived at their station, either had to lower the window if they could and then reach out to open the door from the outside, or they had to wave frantically to try and draw the attention of a porter on the platform and beckon him to let them out before the train moved off again. So when I began fiddling with the door handle, Uncle Tom wasn't in the least perturbed. He just kept on reading peacefully, absent-mindedly mumbling 'Don't play with that door, there's a good boy,' at regular intervals.

Until, that is, he suddenly experienced a huge draught of air and raised his head just in time to see the door swing right out on its huge leather hinges – a 180° swing – with the charge whom he had underestimated, the little boy made of sterner stuff than he knew, his beloved nephew who had been specifically handed over to his care, and his care alone – and at his request! – by his trusting young sister-in-law (the boy's doting mother), hanging on to that door for dear life. I have to concede that his attempt to support me by reaching out of the train and holding on to the seat of my trousers was well-meant, courageous perhaps, even moving in retrospect, but it wasn't in the least helpful to me at the time. I am amazed to this day both at my prescience in first opening the window so that when I fell forward I had something to hang on to, and at my presence of mind in actually grabbing the door even as it swung outward, and at the exact, critical moment. As I swung out with the door, the train was slowing down in readiness to stop at the next station – and fortunately I had also had the sense, despite my tender years, to open the door on the side away from the platform at the next station, so there was no danger of my legs being trapped between door and platform! All in all, it seems to me that I came out of the crisis rather well. Indeed, from my point of view, I single-handedly saved what could have been a very tricky situation, to put it mildly, for my Uncle Tom.

Uncle Tom didn't say very much even at the best of times. Certainly, no word of gladness, let alone of gratitude to me or praise for me, crossed his lips that day as he walked me from the station to our house. He didn't speak at all. He gripped my hand very, very tightly, and didn't let go until, white-faced, he handed me over to my mother, saying only that 'I don't think I'll be taking him anywhere for a while, Dorothy.' Believing simply that I had been more mischievous than usual, but with little idea of what that might mean, my mother didn't ask anything either of him or of me at that moment. It took a while for the whole story to come out in all its details, although I still don't think my assessment of what happened got a fair hearing.

As little children are wont to do, I was growing up. Home had become more of a base to embark from and to return to than a total environment. Much of the free time I had at my disposal, if I were not being taken somewhere by adults, I was spending with other little boys, sharing with them what I knew, discovering what they knew, and casing with them our little universe in search together of new knowledge and experiences and adventures. And of course, the rest of the time, apart from weekends and holidays, I attended school.

CHAPTER 4

School

LIFE AT THE New School was in one important aspect all-of-a-piece with the rest of my young life. Every one of the staff was Welsh-speaking, they were all faithful members of one or other of the chapels in the valley, and my mother's sister was one of the teachers.

There was a strong sense of community in that school – how strong I didn't realise until I had left Garnant and attended another school outside the Valleys. That was partly because all the school's teachers not only lived in our stretch of the valley, but had been born and raised there, and in addition had all taught in the school for a number of years. Having had to begin their teaching careers further afield, they had eventually gravitated back to their native heath and stayed. Several of them had taught the parents of the children they were now teaching, but they all knew the families, backgrounds and actual or potential problems of the children. Through picking up stray bits of my aunt's conversation, I came to understand that those teachers quietly and sensitively went well beyond the call of duty in helping the children in greatest need, both educationally and otherwise.

I had naturally anticipated that having an aunt on the teaching staff would be a great personal advantage for me and would give me a head start on other children in sundry and diverse ways, but it didn't work out that way. Indeed, to my deep disappointment, chagrin and even disgust, my aunt and all the other teachers (who were my aunt's friends socially as well as her colleagues professionally) avoided showing me any favouritism so scrupulously that I was now and then forced to conclude that in bending over so far backward to do so, they were covertly discriminating against me. I was at least not being awarded every brownie point to which I was convinced I was entitled.

The only advantage I can remember that ever accrued to me because one of the teachers was my aunt was that at the end of one school term, after confiscating during that term a number of marbles from various boys who were showing them off to other boys during lessons, she couldn't remember who the boys she had punished in that way were, and so, left with this collection, she took them home and brought them in a bag to our house to give to me.

In our school at that time, marbles were the second most potent male status symbol for boys (penknives were the first). All marbles belonged to one of two categories. First, there were working marbles: the ones you used to compete with in games against other boys. Some of those would be lucky marbles that had a track record of serving their owners well and so would be used oftener than others, becoming, through innumerable frays, battle-scarred veterans. Not only did the marks and chips on these give you greater purchase when you knuckled them, they were signs of character. Those marbles were personalised, were held in affection and esteem, and having earned their owner's loyalty, were never, never, never to be exchanged, no matter how many show marbles or anything else another boy might offer for them. Even to entertain the thought of reducing them to the status of pawns in a commercial transaction would be to reveal oneself as at best a very tacky human being indeed, and at worst someone lacking in basic decency, if not morals.

But there were also show marbles, whose value was purely commercial. They were fancy marbles to be played for, marbles that were put on the line, to be won or lost, to be exchanged for other marbles or for something else, and so definitely not to become attached to. Marbles varied greatly in material – the cheapest were only clay, next up were china marbles, but the very best were of fine glass. They varied also in size, in colour, in outer patterns, and if they were transparent, in inner patterns. Such factors affected their value, and so were matters of great importance to penniless little boys for whom barter was their most regular and reliable means of survival and status. Should you lose that *sine qua non* for a boy, your penknife, ten or twelve good show marbles might at least get you a rusty penknife with a broken blade to use until you might hopefully – after planting a few seeds – get a brand new one next birthday or next Christmas.

The marbles my aunt gave me were a fine collection of the latter kind, which overnight made me perhaps the richest boy in my class. Sadly, however, my excitement turned out to be like the excitement of owning a collection of stolen paintings, since my aunt gave me the marbles on condition that I would never show them to any boy in my class, let alone use them when playing against them, or in making any deals with them!

At the New School I was taught to read and write in Welsh and in English, to add up and to take away, to multiply and to divide. The only other distinctive memories I have of instruction there are of being told stories about incidents in British imperial history. I can't recall ever, since my years at that school, hearing mention of or reading anything at all about Clive of India, or the Black Hole of Calcutta, or the battle between the English General Wolfe and the French General Montcalm for the Heights of Abraham in Quebec (a battle during which both were killed, if my memory serves me), but the stories read to us in the New School about those characters and those events I still remember. Such was some of what our teachers were expected to instil into the minds of us poor children in little Wales in those days. I certainly can't recall being taught much of anything about Wales, its history and its own heroes and literary figures. According to one distinguished Welsh historian, the lack of a Welsh dimension in their education is a factor that enervated the enthusiasm of some influential people in Wales for Welsh self-government at

87

one very significant period in the story of that process during the twentieth century.

The school, however, was where I first encountered on a day-to-day basis a representation not only of children belonging to sections of the community to which I already belonged (my family and neighbours and friends of my parents and those who attended our Sunday School and chapel), but of children from the whole village community. Even in a village such as ours, which was fairly homogeneous, school presented us with an individual and social diversity from which we could hardly fail to learn a great deal, outside of academics, that was new to one as a child. After family life and Sunday School, it was the next important step for me in the process of socialisation.

It was there that I learned, for instance – more subconsciously than consciously at that age of course – about individual human characteristics, about fine physique, good looks, talent, charisma and wealth, and their advantages. They were all ways in which someone or other stood out in my class. There were areas of physical prowess, significant for small boys, in which some classmate or other excelled and was regarded as the champion. Rhys Davies was by far the best fist fighter in the class, Bryan Miller easily the best wrestler, and Sydney Evans was the fastest runner. Those were formidable accomplishments for small boys whose primary gender identity entailed 'not being like girls', and whose secondary gender identity entailed being competitive rather than collaborative. They were accomplishments that already gave those boys quite an edge among their male contemporaries.

The most charismatic of my classmates was Hywel. When he had a mind to and was given only half a chance, he was able, with his ability to tell a story, to hold the class enthralled to a degree that not a single teacher in the whole school was ever able to match, not even the headmaster – in fact, especially the headmaster! Hywel was, above all else, a master at explaining what an innocent, indeed hard-done-by, figure he was in all the predicaments he was always getting into. I'm sure the teachers always suspected that they were going to be taken for a long ride when Hywel began to weave an explanation for something he had done; but he was so likeable, so plausible, and it was always such a pleasant and amusing ride, that any predisposition they might have had to be strict with him the next time he began a narrative would fade away, deflected by his poise when he rose to speak. They would succumb to his coolness and be overwhelmed by sheer curiosity, once Hywel was on a roll.

He was very late arriving at the school one morning. Most of us boys arrived late at school some time or other, some of us regularly. A few of us lived a long way from the school and were late as a result of dawdling for some part of the way rather than leaving home late. Now and then I might befriend a small, pleasant, likeable, roundish stone perhaps, and accepting it as a companion on life's journey for that day, I would with my foot nudge it gently along with me all the way until I reached the school gate, when I would hide it so that no one would know where it was but me, and then I would join up with it on my way out of school and it could accompany me all the way home again. On a day when it was raining I might well look for and find a matchstick or a match-sized twig and float it along with me in a gutter at the roadside, freeing it from an occasional tiny log jam, guiding it safely past a drain. But Hywel lived very close to the school. This day, after he had apologised for his lateness and taken his seat, he was asked by our teacher at that time to stand up and to explain to the whole class why he, who lived just by the school, could possibly be so late, later than everyone else in the class.

He stood up, with a hint of a long-suffering air which seemed to suggest that he didn't think this was really necessary, but that he wasn't, and never had been, the kind of pupil to make life difficult for a teacher and so he was quite prepared to respond to her request, to indulge her whim and acquiesce. He began very slowly – 'Weeell, Miss Evans...' – and with great composure, so that from the very first moment we were all hanging onto his words. He then went on and offered at as great a length as he could possibly manage, the explanation that he had used the chamber pot during the night, but had forgotten after doing so to push it back in again under his bed. When it came time for him to get up in the morning, he had put on the socks his mother had laid out for him while sitting on the bed. Although his intention had then been to put his feet on the floor, he had instead accidentally put them right in the chamber pot and so had had to take those socks off again, call his mother downstairs and ask her to come up so that she could find him another pair of socks. She had put a towel under his feet and told him not to move while she went down again, bringing back with her a bowl of water, soap and another towel so that he could wash his feet – very thoroughly, of course. Only after this was he finally able to put on the fresh pair of socks, finish dressing, take his breakfast, and come to school. And that's why, he concluded, he had arrived late at school! With a contented smile and an air of accomplishment he then sat down.

Hywel had a droll manner of speaking, which made it impossible for us ever to be able to tell whether he was seriously giving what was at least essentially a true explanation, lavishly embellishing only a partial truth, or whether he was creating something completely off the cuff. He relished any opportunity to assure himself, the teacher, and all of us his fellow pupils that he had not lost his talent for genially worming his way out of a predicament. Of course, some of our attention was always given to studying the teacher's expression when Hywel told any of his stories. She would usually be struggling to keep a straight face, but was also, I'm sure, telling herself, as lawyers have to tell themselves now and then if TV courtroom dramas are to be believed, never again to ask anyone a question in public to which she didn't already know the answer – and certainly not Hywel, of all people!

Then there was dark-looking, heavyset, slow-smiling, quiet

Bruno Dalavalle. His father Frank, like most if not all of the original immigrants to the Welsh Valleys from Italy, had been born in Bardi, a village near Parma in the north-east of Italy (the home of Parmesan cheese). I have been told by one of the Dalavalle family that a day is set aside each year in Bardi to welcome home all from the village who have left and gone away to live in other lands, and that easily the most conspicuous Italian accent at that event is the Welsh one!

But Bruno was a first-generation Welsh-born Italian. I wonder what life in a Welsh valley meant for Bruno. World War II at least, when Italy was one of Britain's enemies, must have been a worrying time for all of our Welsh-Italians. Some of those of military age were detained for the duration of the war, just as citizens of Japanese descent in the United States were detained, and I am told there is still a deep, residual anger about that among the Welsh-Italians too. I never heard that the Dalavalles suffered in any way at that time for being Italian. Frank's grandson recently told me that Frank himself had been too old to be of military age, and his sons Joe and Bruno too young. The family did, however, change the name of the business to 'Frank's' after the war began.

The various Italians scattered around our valley and neighbouring valleys met, on Sundays at least, at Mass in the Roman Catholic Church at Ammanford, a few miles away. A priest from a large church in the town of Llanelli 16 miles away came to officiate. There were hardly enough Catholics in our village to justify even a small church building locally. Besides, perhaps the aggressive local Protestant religious climate made raising even a small church for themselves seem an unwise step to our local Catholics at that time. To what extent the community at large in our valley included them in its life is a matter about which I wonder in retrospect whether we should have any concern, although one of the Dalavalles recently told me with enthusiasm that the Italians always felt very welcome and at home in all our Valleys. Whatever that meant for reserved but friendly Bruno, he

91

gave both Italians and Catholics a good name in the eyes of those of us for whom he was our first representative of both species.

Many of the continuing themes of my life began at the New School in Garnant. I never realised when I was young how great a part books and reading would play in my life. The only decent collection of books available to me outside school was in a glass-fronted bookcase in a room in Tad-cu's house. It was a room through which anyone going upstairs from the living room had to pass, but apart from this use as a passage, it was hardly used by anyone. All winter, however, it was heated by a stove fitted into a grate on one of the room's outside walls – a dark brown, coal-burning stove with a door in the front in which there were mica panels through which the fire could be seen. In that room, sunk deep into a comfortable imitation-leather fireside chair, stockinged feet resting wherever on the side of the stove was warm enough for comfort without being so hot as to cause chilblains, I spent many wonderful hours reading *The Count of Monte Cristo*, *Two Years Before the Mast*, *The Three Musketeers*, *Robinson Crusoe*, *A Tale of Two Cities*, *Wuthering Heights*, *The Last of the Mohicans*, *Treasure Island*, *David Copperfield*, *The Deerslayer*, *Uncle Tom's Cabin* and *Tess of the d'Urbervilles*.

These, however, weren't books that had been bought separately. Bookshops weren't common in mining valleys, and for most people who lived in them a journey to some town would be unlikely to include time for a visit to a bookshop. Like many of the books common in the homes of many miners, most of these books belonged to a series that had been offered for sale at a bargain price for regular readers of some daily, national newspaper – in this case the *News Chronicle* – and so they were all bound in the same red cloth cover, they all had their title in the same gold lettering on the spine, and they all had the same print inside. There were in the bookcase, however, some other books that someone in the house had acquired – a few of Welsh poetry (schoolbooks

I think), and one or two Biblical commentaries, but neither one of those kinds of books appealed to me then.

The only other book in that bookcase I can remember reading was one that made a very deep impression on me. I can't recall its title now, but its author was a Dennis Wheatley, and its theme was that during sleep, everyone's spirit, connected to the body by a spiritual tape, embarks on a journey which leads to activities of which the waking person will be unaware. Some people however could train themselves not only to be conscious of the adventures of their own spirits during their wanderings, and to be able to remember them later on waking, but also to follow the ethereal tape of other people's spirits, and discover what they were up to while their bodies slept. In this book, the spirits of people who were good in everyday life became involved in escapades it would horrify them even to hear about during their waking hours, while the spirits of bad people went around doing great and sacrificial good.

It was an intriguing and challenging thesis for a young boy, intriguing and challenging enough to lead me to lie down on my bed more than once and wonder whether I could develop that technique, not only for the thrill of the experience itself, but hopefully also in order perhaps to be able to know whether I myself was a good or a bad person – even, perhaps, to gain some estimate of precisely how good or how bad I really was! I don't suppose I was entirely oblivious either to the prospect of being able to become a moral and spiritual Peeping Tom! There must have been a few people, even then, the nocturnal wanderings of whose spirits I would be curious about.

Anything to read was better than nothing, at any time. One summer's evening when I was nine, Dad sent me to bed early as a punishment for some misdemeanour. It was still light outside, and through my open bedroom window I could hear my friends playing on the street, but active and participatory a child though I was, my confinement turned out not to be the sobering punishment Dad had meant it to be, for at that time Dad was working in the insurance business, and I discovered under my bed a pile of old copies of a trade magazine called *The Insurance Monthly*!

Books have been for me somewhere between a treasure trove and an elixir. I don't hoard them – in fact I try and rid myself of those I suspect I won't read again. I don't even take good care of my books. I handle them carelessly, I turn their pages down, and I mark them. But I have often been so mesmerised in a bookshop that I have bought and brought home a book I already have, and the opportunity to scan the books on shelves in other people's houses is for me an enchantment. I am not at ease on a vacation unless I know there's a book somewhere close at hand that I can turn to and browse through if I want to. The teachers at the New School not only encouraged me to read the Welsh and the English books kept in their own cupboards, but when I had read all those, I would be allowed to go to the classroom next door to look for books which took my fancy in the cupboard of the teacher who taught that class.

However, not all the books I read were pure delight, or even helpful. Sometimes I would read in children's books about children whose lives were very different to mine, children who came from another world, it seemed. Once I read a story about a rich little English girl who lived in some grand Hall or other, and who was horrified one day to discover that another little girl she knew went to bed every night still wearing the vest she had worn all that day! But my sister and I did that too. It was a painful experience as a child to encounter such a harshly critical judgement of the way one lived, one that came with all the authority of the printed word. I felt deeply ashamed, and resolved, I recall, not to mention to anyone what I had read. Nor have I till this moment. There was a further consequence, of course. If one thing I did was considered appalling by someone out there who was important enough to write books, what else in my life might appal the writer of that and other books? I have often asked myself whether or not it was the uncertainty induced in me by one little line in a book that explains why I was for such a long time as an adult, despite receiving a good education, so very, very much more comfortable with working-class people than with others.

Gender difference in my lifetime has been given a new profile, and much of the life given to me to live I have lived with a wife and two daughters, alert and capable women who have taught me – who still teach me – what they think I need to know about relating appropriately to the other gender. But my journey in relating formally to the other gender began at that school.

Even so early there was a certain amount of pairing in the minds of the class, which was roughly related to a hierarchical system. That is, it was assumed that the best-looking and most athletic boy – if he were also reasonably dressed – had property rights on the prettiest girl in the class, as did the second best-looking and most athletic boy have property rights on the second prettiest girl in the class. Our stereotypes of male and female good looks meant that there was no disagreement about who these people were, but all it meant in practice was the connection of the pairs by others in such chalked initials on the lavatory wall as BG xx CD, the rough acceptance of the connection by the pairs concerned, the writing of notes by those girls to those boys, and a manly, disdainful disregard of such notes by the boys!

After the first two or three pairings distinctions began to dissolve and the process became obscure. Some boys and girls hadn't yet awakened to the issues involved, but girls who wanted some part of the action wrote notes to any boy who would read them, while boys who had a need that early in life to express their adoration for some particular female did so by going up to her during playtime and offering to do for her whatever she would like done. We boys didn't aspire far above our status, but neither were we completely without ambition – we aimed as high as we could. My chosen Guinevere, a small, pretty girl with a hairstyle then called a donkey crop – straight hair cut in a horizontal line across the forehead – was demure and proper, but could have done, I see now, with more than a little consciousness-raising in the matter of gender solidarity. What she usually required of me in obeisance was that I go to some other girl on the yard, usually one with thick glasses and a pimply face, and slap her over the head with a soft exercise book. I can't remember being tormented with the ethics of conferring such gratuitous injury on innocent young females, or of getting anything in return for such devotion except the age-old, uncritical male satisfaction of pleasing someone who was just a pretty face. The field of action was confined to one's own class. A whole year was a huge chunk of time when we were children. Children in the class below us were considered babyish, while children in the class above us were virtually senior citizens.

It was at school also that the process of having our national identity defined began for us. In the case of those of us for whom Welsh was the language of the home and family and chapel, which was the majority at our school, we entered school with hardly any English at all. English was at first a language we mostly encountered by learning to read it and write it in class. We were consequently spared most of the errors of spoken English initially – we cut few linguistic corners and we learned very little slang. It was almost a rule of thumb that grammatically, the spoken and written English of young Welsh-speaking children was of a higher standard than that of the non-Welsh-speaking children. However, the reverse side of that process is that colloquial Welsh tended to oust the proper articulations and spellings of correct Welsh. Added to that was the fact that we Welsh-speaking children now and then tended to mispronounce an English word we might never have actually heard uttered – a fact of life that some Welsh-speakers have had to live with even as adults. I remember laughing out loud when one of my daughters spoke of characters in a play, pronouncing the 'ch' as she would in 'charm'. A few months later my wife pointed out to me that I had made the same error in public, speaking of archangels!

But those of us who were first and foremost Welsh speakers quickly learned one profound lesson. We learned that outside our homes and families and chapels, our own language, the language which was such an integral part of our identity – 'the skin of our minds' as the philosopher Wittgenstein called it – ultimately had less clout than English in our own Welsh village. There would be a few pupils in every class who were not only unable to speak Welsh, but for whatever reason, weren't about to learn it either. Although they were in Wales, although Welsh was the prevailing language of the community, it wasn't essential for them to learn it – they could get along without it. It's difficult to believe they didn't lose much in practical and personal growth terms, but we, the mass of their fellow pupils, came to realise that if we were to communicate with them, we would have to do it on their terms. We would have to learn to speak their language.

A certain number of people from England had come to live in the community at one time to work in the coal mines. Most of them had been assimilated into the community and had become fluent Welsh-speakers, but there were some who had remained linguistically apart. Some of those had married others who lived linguistically apart. Others had married a Welsh-speaking spouse but, instead of that dynamic producing, as happened in many cases, a bilingual or even a primarily Welsh-speaking home which blended into the surrounding community, it was linguistic apartness, for whatever reason, which marked the home. It would be mostly the offspring of these kinds of immigrants who couldn't or didn't speak Welsh at school.

The adult Welsh-speakers around us described those who couldn't speak Welsh, and sometimes even those who could but didn't, as English, even when they might have lived all their lives in Wales and came from Welsh stock. We Welsh-speaking children followed the example of our elders in designating all who couldn't or didn't speak Welsh as English – unless they were Italian! That became a contentious matter years later, when minority groups worldwide gained confidence and respect, and the Welsh language became somewhat fashionable – when even Prince Charles studied Welsh in the University College at Aberystwyth for a term, and gained enough proficiency in it to deliver a brief address in Welsh.

Later, having by then learned that English was the language of the post office and the barber's, we were to learn that it was also the language of the glossy comics and the even glossier cinema. There was another world out there, a world which intruded into our Welsh-speaking world, a world in which we needed to find our way in order to survive, a world too in which we wanted to find our way to enjoy its bounty. In the last resort our own language was not essential in that world. By today, largely through the efforts, protests, and sacrifices of a new breed of Welsh-speakers, some young ones especially, Welsh has been increasingly recognised on road signs and on official documents, even in the world of commerce and advertising, and especially in education, but back then English, and English alone, was the language of officialdom.

Whereas some languages approximate each other in the production of sound, the Welsh language and the English language in that respect are inimical to each other. For a native Welsh speaker who doesn't get much practice in doing so, speaking English can be physically uncomfortable and tiring. Like skiing for a novice, it entails using muscles you don't normally use. Later in life I found that to be especially true for me when I had to address large audiences at some length in a formal setting. I seemed to be discovering muscles in my upper lip I didn't know were there. After a while I would feel I was slurring my words, even though when I checked it out on tapes, they would always show that I wasn't.

At one time I gave some thought to discovering what it was about enunciating in Welsh that made it uncomfortable and tiring to speak English, in order to be able to try and reverse the process. A part of it is the great emphasis put on the penultimate syllable of almost every Welsh word (which gives the Welsh accent its sing-song effect). The English language isn't so amenable to a regular pattern of emphasis. Another part is that vowels are never slurred in Welsh as they are in English, nor hard consonants softened as they are in the United States. I asked a colleague in the States one Friday what she intended to do over the weekend. She replied that she would probably do some riding. She looked so unlike any kind of a rider that I pursued the matter. 'What kind of riding? Bicycle? Horse?' 'No,' said she, looking more than a little puzzled, 'ledders!' Understanding that much was a great help years later when giving advice to actors at the Guthrie Theater in Minneapolis who sought my help in producing a Welsh accent to perform some of the parts in Shakespeare's historical plays.

The idiomatic and syntactical structure of your native language can also make speaking another language disconcerting, of course. Celtic languages make great use of prepositions. In Welsh, a woman is not worried – worry is upon her. A man is not emotional – he is under feeling. Again, the basic Welsh sentence begins with the verb, rather than with its subject as in English. In Welsh it's 'Saw the girl the boy', not 'The girl saw the boy.' I once had a nightmare in which, while speaking on a public platform before a very large audience of extremely important people on some grand occasion, I began a sentence in English as I would one in Welsh. It was a sentence that, in my dream, simply couldn't be finished syntactically, with the result that, as time passed, my audience slowly all drifted away and left me there alone, embarrassed and ashamed, but unable to leave the podium because I hadn't finished my sentence, and so had to go on speaking, and speaking, and speaking...

As time went on, even a child in school became aware that speaking English could involve more than a physical, idiomatic or syntactical discomfort. Some young man would go away to work in London, come back home for a visit in six months, and we would hear adults say, 'Harry Owen is home. Have you spoken to him? Doesn't he have lovely English?' 'Lovely English' meant he had learnt to speak English with an accent that not only didn't sound Welsh at all to us (although it might stand out a mile to anyone in England), but to our ears even sounded posh. When I went away at 16 to work in Cardiff, the capital of Wales, many of whose non-Welsh-speaking inhabitants have an accent not exactly noted for being mellifluous, non-Welsh-speakers among my Welsh fellow workers would make friendly but tedious fun of my accent and mimic it. Some native Welsh-speakers would change their accent when they spoke English, for reasons, in their minds, to do with self-esteem. Others felt that if they were to get on in certain areas of life in Wales – let alone in England, should they go to live and work there – they needed to change their accent when they spoke English, and there has been some truth to that.

Sometimes it's not until a burden is lifted from your shoulders that you realise you have been carrying it, and how heavy it has been. It was many years later, at Vineland, in New Jersey in the United States, that I realised how much of a part accent has played in the lives of many of us in Wales. It was there that a woman conversing with me said – well, what she actually said was, 'Gee, I just love that Scoddish accent.' I was already 39 years old, and I walked away from that woman trying to grasp the fact that what she had said was not that accent in general didn't matter, or that my accent in particular was tolerable, but that she loved my accent. That's when I realised how small a part of the world, of England even – for there are those in England who suffer the same tribulation – was the dominant segment of English society that in Britain sets the accent norm. After my personal breakthrough it was very easy to extrapolate from New Jersey and America to Africa and Asia and the Antipodes. Later, I was to enjoy experiences such as sitting in a restaurant in the United States and having a young waitress ask my wife and me if she could hang around our table because 'I just love to hear you guys talk.'

That day in New Jersey, I wanted to dash home immediately to try and lift the burden aspect of accent from my daughters' shoulders. But when I spoke to them about it they weren't ready to hear me. Fiercely proud of their own Welshness, to admit to a Welsh accent being a burden in any sense seemed to them perhaps to admit to being ashamed of their Welshness. Or perhaps it's that they belong to a new generation which doesn't buy at all, or as much, into the harsh accent-value system which was inflicted on me. Nowadays having English, now the world's *lingua franca*, as a second language, with whatever accent, is to belong to most of the rest of the world. But my conditioning in those early years has ensured that I still have to guard against judging a person by his or her English accent.

At that school I also learned about a shameful poverty that went far beyond the poverty that I and many of my fellow pupils shared. Most of us were poor, and memories of that poverty remain with me, some on the surface, in a word or a phrase that comes easily to mind perhaps. Many Welsh words I used frequently as a child are names for things which aren't a part of daily life any more, but even though they aren't a part of my active vocabulary any more, neither have they completely disappeared from my consciousness. One example, *cig gwedder*, is so much a part of my linguistic memory that it must have been a phrase I used frequently at one time. It means 'mutton', the cheapest of all meats when I was a child.

Other memories of poverty are triggered by some happening. Not long ago, in a large food store in London, I saw jars of plum jam, and had to smile. What amused me was that I saw those jars in the gourmet section of the store. The plums out of which the jam in those jars had been made and the other ingredients added may have entitled that jam to be in the gourmet section, but when I was a child plum jam was the staple jam in our house because it cost 10*d.* a 1 lb jar in those pre-decimal days, while a 1 lb jar of strawberry jam (my favourite) cost 12*d.*, a whole shilling! Strawberry jam appeared on our table only on very important occasions – a birthday, or a visit from someone special. Sometimes, however, I would enjoy it somewhere else, at a well-to-do friend's house for instance, should I be invited to stay for tea there!

My childhood poverty has had a small but lasting effect on me. To this day I am, in some ways, a very reluctant spender, sometimes to the point of foolishness. I am comfortable spending larger sums for good value, but in small matters I hold back. I let the petrol in the car's tank go down quite low before filling it again, as if I were saving money in the process. Even were I a multi-millionaire, and badly needed four pairs of socks immediately, I would have trouble buying them all at the same time. What I would be comfortable with would be buying two pairs this month and two the next month.

I know I am not alone in such matters. Recently I spoke to a well-to-do man who lives by the sea, and who told me he had just received the gift of a windsurfing board from his children. He told me how delighted he had been to receive it, since he had wanted one for years. When I asked him why he had never bought one for himself, he smiled ruefully and said he could never have done that – that although he could well afford to do so, somewhere deep within him, and rooted in his upbringing, there was a barrier to that kind of expenditure on himself.

I suppose some minimalist tendencies I have in other areas of my life can also be traced back to a general attitude inculcated in me by the poverty of my childhood. Whereas my wife, when my grandchildren visit us, brings out all the toys we have here for them, my instinct is to bring them out a few at a time. But the time I really come into my own as a minimalist is when I demonstrate to my wife what can still come out of a jar of marmalade that she considers empty, or a tube of toothpaste that she's ready to consign to the rubbish bin. My spirit is more in tune with jars and tubes at that stage than when they are just opened.

But at school I came across another degree of poverty, the poverty of children looked down upon even by the rest of us who were poor. They were the children whose clothes were always ill-fitting and ragged hand-me-downs, children whose noses always ran and who had to use their sleeves to wipe them because they had no handkerchiefs, children who weren't kept clean by their parents. Those children were singled out for attention by health officials, a doctor or a nurse, when they visited the school. Sometimes lice would be found in the hair of one or more of them, and they would be sent home immediately. My parents knew they were not wealthy, but it was a matter of immense and aggressive pride for them that no one should be able to think for one moment that they didn't have a clean home, or didn't keep their children clean.

The children singled out for attention by school health visitors were usually the children of large families – children with nine or ten brothers and sisters. There was oftener than not some other factor or factors too: a father who drank heavily, a mother with too little support and too worn out, and perhaps otherwise unable to cope. The rest of us avoided those children like the plague on the school yard, and we would be unwilling to sit next to them in the classroom. As children do, we made our unwillingness very clear, with wrinkled noses and frowns and glares and hurtful comments. We looked down on them, and made fun of them. It was a vicious beginning to life, and the memory of the shame I saw in the eyes of one pretty little girl wearing her older brother's jacket when she was sent home one day by a health visitor has stayed with me. Yet none of us, except the richest boy in the class, had enough self-assurance to be openly sorry for our poorer, defenceless classmates and to speak up for them.

Some children were different in other ways. There was the big, strong, clumsy, unattractive, masculine girl whose pleasure it was – egged on by other girls – to scare the wits out of small boys by catching them, taking them to one of the outside toilets, holding their heads down inside the bowl, and flushing it without getting their hair wet. When I was the recipient of her attention, I always felt more sorry for her than angry with her. I was already beginning to learn at school about unkindness and discrimination and injustice, even cruelty, particularly in regard to girls.

At school we also discovered that yet another kind of human

being existed, creatures that belonged to a universe completely different from the universe in which any of us lived, even the boy whose father owned a store. They were the gentry of our part of the world, and many of the roads, streets and buildings of the village bore their names. I went to Sunday School in Stepney Hall, Tad-cu lived on Stepney Road, and in 1935, on the twenty-fifth anniversary of the coronation of King George V, Lady Stepney visited our school, requested the headmaster to give us children a half day's holiday to celebrate the event (he did), and presented each of us with a mug which had on it pictures of King George and Queen Mary, the dates of the coronation and anniversary, and 'Presented by Lady Stepney'.

During my childhood, ongoing social changes meant that these larger-than-life people were fading into the background. But a new larger-than-life set of people was fast becoming the new stars in the firmament of many people, not only in little Wales, but the whole world over.

CHAPTER 5

The Cinema

IN ADDITION TO the school, there were two other powerful institutions that were very influential in my world when I was a child, and one was the cinema, which in the Valleys then we spoke of as 'the pictures'. The cinema, certainly compared to the other two institutions, was a latecomer on the social scene, but it figured so hugely in the lives of my generation in the Western world that it would be difficult to overestimate its effect on us all, even on those of us who visited the cinema only very rarely – or not at all.

In almost every village of any size in the Valleys, there was at least one cinema. Possessing a cinema of its own was a measure of the significance of, and therefore a necessity for the pride of, any village, let alone any town. In the larger villages and the towns there might even be two or three cinemas.

The Valleys of my childhood were festooned with cinemas. On dark winter evenings, the light which escaped from their open front doors, and which poured down from lamps embedded in the ceilings of the porches which extended out from them, cast a bold radiance on the pavement in front of them. Many of the cinemas were garlanded on the outside with brightly-coloured bulbs, which were beacons heralding warmth and comfort to dispel some of the gloom in small, misty villages on cold, damp nights. But the cinemas themselves were invitations the year round to souls tyrannised by the mundane and the drab to escape any dreariness for a while.

All the cinemas had their own proper names. Privately-owned cinemas were sometimes known affectionately by the names of their owners – Vince's, or Sam's. But most of them had their own proper, pretentious names which laced our pedestrian, proletarian lives with a dash of incongruous bourgeois flavour: the Palladium, the Lyric, the Odeon, the Grand, the Pavilion, the Hippodrome, the Capitol, the Forum, the Regal, the Lyceum, the Astoria. The classical flavour of those names made them redolent, of course, of Ancient Greece and Rome, like highlights in a guided tour of antiquity, although not many of us could make the connection.

Some of them were broken down, ramshackle places. A few of those were even referred to as fleapits, and some would swear to the appropriateness of that appellation, but I suspect that in the case of at least some such places, their fleas were psychological ones – although those were quite as capable of producing an itch that needed to be scratched as the real thing! Real or not, unless he enjoyed taking off every single item of his clothing so that he could be minutely inspected there and then, and subjected to a very thorough and painful shampoo and scrubbing, it paid any small boy with a mother as poor but proud as mine was to concentrate hard on not scratching any itch, whatever its cause, on returning home from a cinema reputed to be a fleapit. Some people would not be caught dead in such a cinema, but I never heard of any cinemas in those days, even those with the worst of all reputations, closing down due to a lack of customers.

Yet despite the economic harshness of the times, many of the cinemas were grandiose palaces. Some of the bigger and better cinemas in the Valleys were built, owned and run by public bodies, even by trade unions, and those had politically-correct names such as, in my part of the world, the Welfare Hall in Gwaun-Cae-Gurwen, and the Public Hall in Brynamman. Some of these were originally intended to contribute much more to the lives of their communities than merely show movies and make a good profit while doing so. Some of them, such as the Public Hall in Brynamman, which housed a library and a billiard room as well as a cinema, have managed to retain all their original functions even to this day, but in time most of the others became cinemas almost exclusively, before finally closing down as populations decreased and television and dining out took their toll.

The building which housed the cinema in our village was called the Workmen's Hall. The raising of the Workmen's Hall was a stunning political statement for its day, a statement made by the organised working men of the community. It was a statement about the shape of things to come, the direction of the community's life, and the readiness and ability of the working men to guide it. It was a statement all the more powerful for being made at a time of very, very great hardship for them. Paid for by Union funds put together by subscriptions from miners' wages over time, it cost £12,000, in 1927 – just one year after the General Strike of 1926. That Strike was a defining moment, and remains a point of reference for the older British Trade Unionists.

The Strike itself, however, was but the tip of the iceberg. The years leading up to it had been a lean period for the British

Garnant Workmen's Hall and cinema

working class at large, but especially for the coal miners. With the development of coal-mining in other countries too, and the decline of competitiveness in the British coal industry, there had been a devastating loss of overseas markets for British coal. The coal owners had placed the burden of the crisis on the miners by reducing wages and extending the working day, until finally the Trades Union Congress had called a General Strike throughout Britain in support of the miners. The official strike lasted nine days, but the withdrawal of labour in general continued long after the official strike had ended. It continued longer among coal miners than other workers, and longer among the coal miners of South Wales than among most other coal miners. The Workmen's Hall was planned, its foundations laid, the building erected, at a time of hungry miners on street corners, of soup-kitchens in chapels, of women fainting because they were giving their meals to their children, of children barefoot, and of high infant mortality rates.

As well as being a political statement, the raising of the Workmen's Hall was also a socio-religious statement. Hitherto, the largest building in Garnant had been the largest chapel, Bethel Newydd. Now Bethel Newydd was dwarfed by a new and secular temple. Before the raising of the Workmen's Hall you could go up to the top of the Black Mountain, look down at the valley, and the building that stood out most conspicuously was Bethel Newydd. Should you want to point something out to a companion from the mountain top, the easiest way would be to start by pointing out Bethel Newydd and work from there. But after 1927 the place to start would be with the Workmen's Hall. Even Bethel Newydd, after the raising of the Workmen's Hall, became the long, grey, slate roof on the same road, and the same side of the road, as the Workmen's Hall, but a little to the right of it.

Nor was it only a matter of the size of the new building. Previously, it had mainly been the chapels that had offered a home for all kinds of meetings in the community, and for various cultural events. That had meant certain obvious and understandable limitations. Sometimes the limitations were to do with the nature of the event. Some cultural activities, oratorios for instance, took their place naturally in a chapel – only chapel choirs would perform those anyway – but operettas didn't. Political meetings were sometimes held in a chapel, but that depended on what kind of a political meeting it was, and on the support of the minister of the chapel and its lay officers. Sometimes the limits pertained to facilities or size. Not all plays were regarded as appropriate for the chapel – comedies especially, but they might be performed in the vestry which every chapel had. The vestry was below, behind or at the side of the chapel, and if behind or at the side might be attached to the chapel or free standing. Whatever its location, the chapel vestry would often have a small stage, but space for props and for the actors to make up and change was very limited. The vestry would also be much smaller than the chapel, so in order to accommodate the number of people who might want to see it, a popular play might have to be performed on up to four nights in succession – quite a demand on the time and energies of an amateur company.

More significantly however, until the Workmen's Hall was built, the chapel was the only large space in the community, and an increasing number of people, more than chapel people probably realised, felt uncomfortable in the ambience of a chapel. While that situation continued, in practice many were excluded from some events – even events sponsored by organisations outside the chapel and which were meant to be open to the community at large.

The committee which managed the Workmen's Hall then didn't have to consider some matters the leaders of a chapel might feel obliged to consider. In addition, the Hall had a grandiose stage, rich velvet curtains which were operated mechanically, footlights and spotlights, a backstage area with sets and changing rooms, plush seats and even an orchestra pit. Here, in a neutral space, was a much more than adequate and comfortable public home for many things cultural and social, for drama festivals and light opera and Welsh concerts, for public presentations and community celebrations. All these could be accommodated in the luxury of the Workmen's Hall without limitations or constraints of any kind, and before large crowds, including people who might not feel completely at home in any chapel. Here too was a forum for public meetings – including political ones of all kinds, which could be held there even on Sundays. The social hegemony of the chapel, which until then had hosted, served, fostered and influenced so much of the community's social life, had come to a final end. The Workmen's Hall was the definitive sign, and it was written in handsome stone.

In the case of the Workmen's Hall, as in the case of other such halls, despite the most worthy and altruistic social and cultural intentions of those whose dream it was, there weren't enough other kinds of social and cultural occasions to make great, year-round use of it apart from showing films, so most nights it simply functioned as a cinema. In time, therefore, the Hall came to be regarded as a cinema which was sometimes used for other functions also – functions which were a cause of annoyance for those hooked on their weekly or bi-weekly movies, and who suffered withdrawal symptoms when deprived for a few nights.

There can hardly have been ever before in all of human history a cultural success so instantaneous and spectacular in any society as the success of movies everywhere in the Western world. Certainly the crowds that wended their way home from the Workmen's Hall after a show had ended were from the very beginning greater in numbers almost every weeknight than the crowds that wended their way home from the chapel on almost any Sunday night. This too was a statement, a sign of the times. An era was coming to an end.

The Workmen's Hall was a golden fairy-tale palace. The floors of its foyer and stairs were covered with thick carpets, subdued lights gently caressed walls decorated with moulded designs, and inside the plush tip-up seats were as far removed from the austerity and discomfort of chapel pews as they could possibly be. And every wall space was splashed with large framed technicolour portraits of handsome, moustached, square-jawed men, and of glossy, glamorous women.

On Saturday nights I would usually leave home around 4.30 p.m., 4*d.* in my hand, to catch the 'first house' at the Workmen's Hall at 5 p.m. (the 'second house' began at 8 p.m.). With one penny I bought sweets from Ellis at Siop Danybryn on the way. (Ellis was something we were short of in our village – he was a celebrity. Hadn't he shared a trench in France in World War I with the film star Basil Rathbone, who became the definitive movie Sherlock Holmes, and didn't he have on a sideboard in the living room behind the shop – some privileged people had been allowed to see it and so could bear witness to it – an autographed photograph of Basil inscribed 'To My Friend Ellis' to prove it?)

My choice of sweets was usually a pennyworth of large, hard, virtually unbreakable and almost everlasting toffees wrapped in brown and yellow papers. They were so big I could hardly get one of them into my mouth, but that was a problem I struggled manfully with every time it arose, and while not wanting to seem boastful, and conceding that the memory can deceive at times, I think I can safely claim that I never completely failed to overcome it. They were called Radiance Toffees, and I could get eight for a penny.

But if you chose to, for the same price Ellis would hand you a small piece of wood, like a matchstick, and a small board full of tiny holes with a minute roll of paper in each one. With the piece of wood you pushed one of the rolls of paper out of its hole – holding the board over the counter, as per Ellis' instruction, for should the paper fall to the floor, you would have to get on your hands and knees and look for it. This would hold up the line of people behind you, who were in a hurry, for they also wanted to buy sweets, cigarettes too perhaps, to take with them to the same show as you were going to, and Ellis wasn't the kind of man to want anyone to feel too pressed for time to stay and make a transaction. Then Ellis opened out the roll of paper, which told you which sweets you would get for your penny. In fairness to him, Ellis would always ask you if you wanted to see the paper yourself, but no one ever did. Balancing the choice of something I knew for sure that I liked, against the excitement of mystery and the unknown, was a major weekly dilemma. It was the prototype, the first precursor, of a kind of decision to be repeated in innumerable restaurants here, there and everywhere throughout my adult life. Now and then, life was to demand such a decision on issues greater than what to eat, of course.

In the Workmen's Hall I would sit at the very front, where half a dozen rows of wooden double seats rested on a flat floor made of boards which covered the orchestra pit when movies were shown. Unaccompanied small children, mostly boys, were admitted for only 2d. to those wooden seats, but the people sitting in the rising plush seats behind were protected even from having to view the rapscallions in this section by a high, wooden partition.

The first intimation of the lowering of the lights, which coincided with the slow opening of the curtains on the stage, was always a magical moment. Hitherto the whole lit-up place would have been a buzz of conversation, people chatting with people in front of them, and those in front turning around to carry on their end of the dialogue, but from that moment onward no one dared speak a word – all conversation was required to cease, and cease it did. The hush was audible, all ears would be tuned in to the sound from the speakers and all eyes would focus on the silver screen. Attention could not be more rapt.

Cigarette smoke hung heavily in the dark air the whole time, its curling blue-grey streamers illuminated by the light beamed down to the screen from the projection room at the back of the balcony, and it never occurred to any of us then to think there was anything wrong with that. Years later, watching a movie in a cinema in good old progressive Amsterdam, I sensed that there was something different in the experience this time, something missing from the total event. It took me a while to realise that I was for the first time in a cinema where smoking was prohibited.

The whole show would be screened once on Monday, Tuesday and Wednesday nights, and then it would be completely changed for Thursday, Friday and Saturday nights, with two shows on Saturday night. The weekly programme for the shows at each cinema in our and neighbouring villages – the titles of the B-movies and the main feature movie and the names of the stars of the main feature movie – were displayed prominently on billboards here and there in each village: the name of the cinema at the top followed by the dates in blue, the titles of the movies in red, and the names of the stars in dark blue. The sight of a man on a ladder with a bucket of paste and a long brush putting up new posters over old ones on a billboard was a common part of the local scene then.

As the villages were close to each other, with good bus services, it was easy to go to the cinema every night of the week without seeing the same show twice, and there were those who boasted of doing that – although some went to see the same movie in the same place twice in the same week. I was allowed to go only once a week, to that 'first house' on Saturday night, and when the whole show had come to an end, the curtain had been closed and the lights turned up, we who sat in the tuppenny seats were ushered out briskly and unceremoniously so the floor could be swept and the wooden chairs arranged tidily again for the 'second house'.

After the show I would make my way home back up the valley, accompanied by a friend or two, and always encompassed by a procession of villagers who had been to the same show. Since the Workmen's Hall was at the lower end of the village, the procession always comprised almost all of that show's audience. We filled the narrow main street from side to side, enveloped in a sense of freedom and a feeling of fuzzy, warm companionship. It was a Saturday evening, we had all been out, and whatever we had watched had taken us far away from the mundane in our lives. We had now been let loose again but we were still on a high. We had gone to the cinema separately, but we all left together. We might walk in small separate groups, but a feeling of camaraderie hung heavily on the night air. We had all been sitting cosily together in the dark for some two and a half hours, which was still a comparatively new social experience for many of us, and the finale of that two and a half hours would have been a full-length film, which, be it sad or joyful, serious or comic, a drama or an adventure or a Western or a musical, would have moved us in some way, so that it would be as people somehow bound together by that shared audio-visual and emotional experience that we would wend our way homeward.

There were several fish and chip shops along the road, and those who served in them would be waiting for us, poised to minister to our particular exodus from the Workmen's Hall, with chips, fish, pies, rissoles and sausages-in-batter warmed at the ready, and they themselves, like a football team before a kick-off, psyched up for the onrush of customers. We all had our favourite shop, and as we arrived at each, a goodly number would drop out of the procession. I would walk fairly quickly away from the Hall, wending my way through the crowd to get to Glanmor's chip shop. Glanmor's was the converted front room of a semi-detached house, and wasn't very big, so it was important for a small boy to get there before it became too crowded. At Glanmor's, I would work my way to the counter to spend my last penny on a portion of chips, served in a greaseproof-paper bag wrapped in a piece of newspaper by Glanmor or his attractive auburn-haired wife. Having given my order, in Welsh, I would be served. I would sprinkle salt and vinegar on my chips, I would hand over my penny, take my open packet of chips and make my way from the oppressive steam and heat generated inside by both the food frying and the crowd, and out to the fresh night air. Young boys and girls older than I was would gather outside the shop after being served, girls sitting on the front window sill and boys standing, and they would chat, joke and flirt as they ate. The night was still young for them, but I had to make my way home once I had been served or Mam would worry, and I ate my chips as I went. Then all Mam had to do when I arrived home was to get me undressed and washed, put me into my pyjamas, give me a glass of milk, and then she could send me off to bed, to relive on a satisfied stomach the wonders I had experienced that night!

On rare occasions Mam would go on a shopping expedition to Swansea, and sometimes she would take my sister and me with her. After she had finished her shopping, she might take us to the Plaza cinema there as a treat. As regards the number of seats, the spaciousness, the style and the ambience, even the provincial grandeur of the Plaza made the Workmen's Hall seem very small potatoes indeed, on the inside and the outside. The Plaza even had a grand café on the first floor, with a smartly dressed woman to guide people to a table, waitresses in black dresses and white pinafores and white caps, wicker chairs, shiny glass-topped tables, paper serviettes and menus. But we never went to the café. For me, eating at the Plaza café would have to await the day in my late teens when I wanted to impress a girl from another valley on my first date with her, and not without a degree of nervousness chose the not-cheap Plaza café as our meeting place.

At the Plaza, after the B-movie, there would be an interval during which the lights would be raised a little. Music would be heard, from a great distance it seemed at first, the sound of it gradually growing in volume until finally an organ, ablaze from the inside with a rainbow of coloured electric bulbs, would surface majestically from the floor in front of, but a little way back from, the screen, until it came into full view like an alien spaceship. An organist wearing a white bow and black tails would be seated at the console, and when the organ had been raised to its full height, it was high enough for all there to see his feet move on the pedals – the part of his performance which most intrigued the musically uncouth among us. When he had finished the piece he was playing, he would casually turn around, throw one leg gracefully over the organ bench, face the peasants now before him and greet us all with a beguiling, personalised smile and a princely flourish of his hand, before turning back again to face the console and to bewilder us with his repertoire of popular music and songs – some of which the audience would sing. Finally, he would turn to us again, wave us a sad goodbye, the sound would begin to subside, and the organ would slowly descend, sped on its way to its underworld lair with our rapturous applause, until it had completely disappeared. Then, although we had enjoyed the interlude immensely, we would return, refreshed, to apply ourselves diligently to the infinitely more serious business, of course, of screen-watching.

Each show in the Workmen's Hall consisted of a B-movie, a newsreel, promotional clips of coming movies, advertisements, and the main feature. Many B-movies were cowboy films, featuring tough guys – real men – such as Buck Jones, Ken Maynard, and Tom Mix. In time all of these were displaced, to the disgust of every right-thinking boy, by the singing, guitar-strumming, sequinned and generally overdressed poseurs Gene Autry and Roy Rogers, whose personalities were overshadowed by those of their horses. But some B-movies were about gangsters and crooks, starring such as the young Humphrey Bogart, James Cagney, George Raft, Sydney Greenstreet and Peter Lorre, and to sort out any and all gangsters and crooks on his own – more or less – in the process of defending society and making the world a safer place for decent people to live in, the good old honest cop, Lloyd Nolan.

We were not the most sophisticated of audiences at the Workmen's Hall. It was common there, at least during the 'first house', to cheer heroes when they were being heroic, and to boo and hiss villains when they were being villainous – but only during the B-movies. It was as if we were all together outwardly limbering up our sensibilities in preparation for a more interior, a deeper, more intense emotional response to the main feature.

Over the years one came to feel that some of the actors were almost personal acquaintances. When I became older, I felt so indebted at one stage in my life to Gary Cooper for the many wonderful hours of fine entertainment with which he had provided me – culminating in *High Noon* – that it seemed not totally unreasonable to wonder whether, in the sad event that he should die before I did, I might not consider attending his funeral. But all the heroes at the Workmen's Hall were ten feet tall – literally, as viewed by us small boys from our wooden seats right under the screen at the very front of the Hall.

The newsreels would introduce us to the world at large, but with a National Geographic quality of innocence. Much of it was a stirring view of the world from the standpoint of good old British imperialism – our largesse here, how much the natives loved us there, laughing troops giving chocolates to grateful black children here, grand military parades there, British sporting successes in everything and everywhere. And, always, the royal family: planting trees, going to church at Balmoral, kissing sick children in hospitals, launching ships, attending weddings, having their children baptised at Windsor, visiting the colonies, and sometimes just standing together and smiling from the balcony of Buckingham Palace at their adoring, flag-waving subjects below.

Previews reminded us each week that no matter how greatly we would enjoy the show that evening and despite whatever last week's promotional preview might have told us, nevertheless – sadly perhaps, but as a matter of simple, incontrovertible fact: the previews proved it – we were all there a week too early, and so if we were to see the most romantic, dramatic, magnificent, heart-stopping, terrific, stupendous, colossal, monumental something-or-other of all, we would have to come back again next week.

Advertisements weren't aimed at small boys, so I remember nothing about them, except that that's when heavily made-up young women in some kind of uniform would walk around in the darkness, bearing in front of them a tray hanging from a strap around their necks, inside which there was a small light which shone on their wares – ice cream, cartons of orange juice, sweets, chocolates and cigarettes.

Then, of course, the long-awaited big feature. This was when people who had never been anywhere or seen or done much, who read very little perhaps, and had virtually no experience of theatre, were introduced to sights and sounds and happenings beyond their wildest imaginations. To desert sands and boundless prairies, to marshlands, swift rivers, tropical jungles, South Sea islands and mighty oceans. To floods, famines, earthquakes, volcanoes, typhoons and hurricanes. To lonely homesteads, small towns and great cities. To rattle-snakes rattling, lions roaring, whales spouting, and elephants trumpeting. To cowboys on cattle drives and armies on the march, kings reigning, cardinals machinating and presidents presiding. To magnificent choreography and smooth musicals, to mutinies and revolutions and wars. To planes with the petrol gauge showing zero, flying crazily amidst thunder and lightning while the pilot looked in vain through thick clouds and teeming rain for some makeshift landing strip. To luxury liners sinking and leaving nothing but a dozen incompatible male and female survivors and an inexperienced young officer to face the harsh rigours of hunger, thirst and sunstroke on a lifeboat at sea. At no time before, anywhere in the world, had ordinary people – or any other kind of people – been offered such a gourmet visual diet, for such a small outlay, and for six nights a week. It was a massive, incalculable phenomenon.

I know some things those movies did to us. They helped us Welsh-speaking children learn English – including American English! One day, many years later, pouring fuel into my car on the forecourt of a gas station in the United States, I thought quietly to myself how disastrous it would be were I ever to say 'gas' to my friends in Wales instead of 'petrol'. At the very least I would be ostracised from the best Welsh social circles for a time – perhaps forever. Then it dawned on me that 'gas' had in fact been one of my earliest English words, picked up from B-movies about Chicago gangsters, as in 'Step on the gas!' How much British English I also imbibed from staring quietly at a screen in a dark cinema and wanting so much to understand everything that was going on, I shall never know, but it must have been a very great deal.

Some of the English I picked up, like the use of OK, was American slang which our parents thought they ought to discourage strongly – and did, but they were fighting a losing battle, and well they knew it, for they themselves were not immune to the seductiveness of the language and images of the world of movies. My mother would sometimes say about a man wearing an ill-fitting suit or walking with a funny gait that he looked 'a real Charlie', and should I eat too many sweets her warning to me might well be that I would soon end up like Fatty Arbuckle. In addition to all its other effects on our community, the world of the cinema became for us a source of words, similes and metaphors in our daily speech.

The cinemas themselves, or to be more precise, their balconies, effected a great change in the dating patterns of young people. The cinema in Glanamman (sometimes called Sam's Show, in reference to its owner, and sometimes the Rink, referring to its former function, but never called by its proper name, the Palace) had no balcony, and so wasn't the most popular movie venue among young people. Garnant's cinema had a balcony, so it was fine – unless, that is, you suffered from the slightest degree of vertigo, for the Workmen's Hall, built on a steep slope, had the sheerest, most frightening cinema balcony I have ever come across. Walking down the aisle to your row was like driving down some of San Francisco's streets, and when you reached your row and left the aisle to walk over to your seat – past people who were sitting there already perhaps, giving you little room to manoeuvre – your feet would be at the level of the necks of the people sitting in the row in front, and there was simply nothing to lean on or hold on to on either side if you felt you were about to lose your balance. The Welfare Hall at Gwaun-Cae-Gurwen, on the other hand, had a balcony with a civilised incline, and if my memory serves me, it could boast of a few double seats in the very back row of the balcony!

I don't know first hand what problems were involved for young people in making secret assignations and keeping trysts before the advent of the cinema, in a village where everyone knew everyone, where there was always someone at home, when teenagers couldn't drive and even if they could, wouldn't be able to get hold of, let alone own, any kind of car. But whatever the problems might have been, the balconies of cinemas solved them all for my generation of young people. Boys and girls could now meet without even acknowledging one another in public. A boy who had his eye on a girl simply went inside the cinema with his friends, sat with them in the balcony until the lights were lowered, then changed seats by pre-arrangement with the girl who was sitting next to the light of his life for that evening, and the rest was up to the gods. Usually he would return to sit with his friends as the movie was ending – to the accompaniment of hisses from those who might be there actually to see the movie, although they would only be a very small percentage of those sitting in the balcony!

Just as sitting in the balcony at all had to wait until one was getting enough pocket money to be able to afford it, so meeting a girl outside the cinema was for when one was getting enough pocket money to risk the possibility of being expected to pay for two tickets, and for when one was serious enough about the girl to be ready to pay that much if the worst came to the worst! Meeting a girl outside the cinema was a sign of commitment anyway. Commitment or not, most young people in my village in those days experienced their first fumbling, clumsy, hesitant kisses, learned to home-in without lights on the lips of someone from the opposite sex, did their basic course in courtship, upstairs in the darkness of the balcony either of our own Workmen's Hall, or of the Welfare Hall in Gwaun-Cae-Gurwen.

A hierarchical seating system operated even in the balcony of the cinema, and in this case it served a useful function, of which parents of young people were well aware. Older couples – 19? 20? – didn't want to be embarrassed by being watched by much younger couples, among whom there might well be a brother or sister, or at least a cousin, so they commandeered the back seats. The younger couples had to sit in front of an older brother or sister perhaps, who might well have been instructed by their knowing parents to keep an eye on their younger sibling. It was a brake on callow passion. As for the older ones, there was always a marshal or two among the usherettes, self-appointed guardians of public morality who, if they actually saw steam rising, would wait for a quiet, tense moment in the movie, walk down as far as the row in question, then shine a powerful torch across in the direction of the couple concerned and stage-whisper some very loud and discouraging words.

The cinema also to some extent diminished for those who frequented them any sense they might have of general isolation. Movies brought the outside world not only to villages ensconced in valleys and some distance from the nearest fair-sized town, but to provincially circumscribed towns some distance from the nearest city, let alone some great metropolis. In doing so, villagers, townies and urbanites were together quietly and uniformly brought along to belong a little more to the great outside world, the global village that was even then coming into being. It was for many the first step in the process of globalisation. Much of that outside world was America, of course, but not all of it by any means.

The cinema contributed to diminishing cultural isolation too. When they sat down to watch a movie in the Workmen's Hall, people from Garnant were viewing a presentation that people throughout the English-speaking world would view. There was also a sense of literally getting the best, for once, even in the Valleys. Plays and operas performed locally might not be up to the quality of plays put on in London's West End or operas at Covent Garden, but the movies we saw were exactly the same movies as the movies seen anywhere else in the world. Not only was it often a feast fit for kings and queens, it was precisely the same feast that a king or a queen would partake of were they to see that movie. The downside was that that also diminished for many their appreciation of live entertainment, particularly that offered by local amateur talents. While cinema-goers tended to accept Hollywood's presentations uncritically, their appetite for the best offerings of people they knew personally became jaded, especially if what was being offered were a play or a musical that Hollywood had already produced. After hearing a very young Jeanette MacDonald sing 'An Indian Love Song', a not-so-young Bronwen Griffiths singing it for the local light opera company rather suffered by comparison – especially on the high notes!

Some of what interested us small boys in the movies we reproduced on the school playground. We would dash hither and thither holding the handle bars of imaginary motor cycles or turning the steering wheels of imaginary sedans, pretending to be cops; or we would lope around slapping our sides, pretending to be cowboys – unless our low position in the class's male hierarchy denied us those privileges and forced us instead to be crooks or Indians. Of course, all this also affected the lists of toys we made in the letters we put up the chimney for Santa Claus to read, for unlike our fathers when they were children, we boys would include on our lists cowboy hats, red neckerchiefs, gun belts, sheriff's stars, revolvers (preferably repeaters, with explosive caps) and rifles, or headdresses, bows and arrows and quivers, and sometimes even automatics and tommy guns.

The universal appeal and the uncritical acceptance of the cowboy myth in particular was amazing. I remember that Mam one day took me with her when she visited a woman to sympathise with her because her son, who was my age, had just died, although I can't remember from what. The woman was so moved that Mam had brought me with her that she wanted to give me something her son had owned for me to remember him by. She left the room and in a minute returned, bringing with her two toy metal revolvers, one brand new, one chipped and otherwise marked with use. She explained that she wanted to keep his best gun, but that she would be glad if I would accept the other gun to remember him by. That seemed to make sense at the time – simply a nice gesture – and it was that of course; but looking back at it over the years, that a mother living in a Welsh mining valley should, in memory of her dead son, want to keep for herself and to give to a little boy something we all knew about only through the world of American cowboy movies, and a gun at that, is a transaction which has a bizarre aspect to it culturally.

Movies had an effect on many kinds of adult behaviour of course. They introduced Valleys people to, among other things, the great outside word of trends, styles and fashions that they were implicitly invited to copy. It affected them as parents: although my mother hadn't bought it for that reason, she wasn't offended when some people said that in one of my suits I looked exactly like Freddie Bartholomew. Other mothers had their daughters wear their hair in Shirley Temple ringlets, and arranged for them to learn tap-dancing, which became quite a craze for some girls in the Valleys for a time. Then there were the likes of Frederic March, Brian Donlevy, Herbert Marshall, Don Ameche, Ralph Bellamy, Myrna Loy, Ginger Rogers, Loretta Young, Paulette Goddard, Barbara Stanwyck, romantic denizens of a slick world not short of material for creating wonderful dreams to languish in, and sometimes to identify them permanently with some of their roles. I still visualise Delilah as Hedy Lamarr.

Young Welsh coal miners grew George Brent-style moustaches, and in their fantasies would converse, no doubt, in a low, husky Ronald Colman voice (with a Charles Boyer accent?), as they escorted some elegant, willowy femme fatale to a nightclub, and bantered, danced and flirted with her until dawn. Meanwhile young (and not so young) Welsh women not only had dreams in which they played the femme fatale to the Franchot Tones, Clark Gables and Dick Powells of the movies' firmament, but wore Deanna Durbin hats (Carmen Miranda's headgear never caught on in our valley) and imitated Claudette Colbert's fringe for a while. And still what they saw of the stars on the screen wasn't enough to satisfy people's desires. They craved to know all there was to know about their private lives, and to satisfy the demand there were movie magazines for adults, with large cut-out pictures, and for children there were comics featuring Laurel and Hardy, Tarzan and Sabu – and they all sold well in our Valleys!

Overall, did the close attendance of so many of us on that celluloid world contribute to our lives or detract from them? Many adults went to the cinema on a regular basis, as I did on Saturday nights, no matter what movie was being shown, and the cinemas were there for them, every night of the week. That was a part of the early and continuing success of cinemas – in the days before television, what other form of recreation was available six nights a week, rain or shine, winter and summer! Watching some movies was unquestionably a waste of time and money for anyone, although whether those of us who watched those would have done anything better with the time and money we would have saved by not going is a moot point.

I have groaned over the years at things I have learned about some of the people who have in one way or another wielded great influence in the film industry. There was the man, basically an accountant, who for many years controlled most of the British film industry. He set British film-making back for a long, long time because he simply wanted to churn out guaranteed moneymakers such as Norman Wisdom comedies and the 'Doctor' series, and had not the slightest grasp at all of such matters as art, creativity or integrity. Some film-makers were flawed in less conspicuous ways. One was the director who made Gregory Peck commit adultery in the movie *On The Beach*, although that didn't take place in the novel of that name by Neville Shute on which the movie was based. The director's defence against Shute's angry protest was that Peck's character's wife in the film was dead at the time, so it wasn't adultery – even though he didn't know she was dead! Then there was the one time pugilist, the physically large John Huston, a film-maker of stature too, yet who was unable, hard though he tried eventually, to transcend in his films the white male macho theme. Even when he made Toulouse-Lautrec his hero, the theme was still male domination of women, albeit artistic domination in that movie. And there was what films did to Indians, women and blacks, and so often still does to Asians.

The cops-and-robbers and cowboys-and-Indians films were morality plays, fine for children perhaps, and for the child in all of us. However, those of us in Wales whose identity was bound up with the Welsh language didn't understand then, just as Native Americans in the United States who cheered the cowboys in cowboys-and-Indians movies didn't realise that with a looking-back-and-inward rather than looking-forward-and-outward Welsh-speaking mentality, without any prospect then of a government using our own language, and with our history marginalised even in the education system, we ourselves were really the Indians, and not the cowboys we wanted to be on the school yard.

As these morality plays became a regular part of most adults' diet, the over-simplification of life in them can't have done too much good, and may have harmed sensibilities if watched uncritically, as most people surely did this new medium. I wonder too whether the light-hearted approach to marriage in so many Hollywood movies in the thirties didn't contribute to, as well as reflect, the shallow understanding of commitment in marriage which later became a trend. I wonder too whether the standardisation of youthful good looks didn't dehumanise us all a little. And I wonder whether all the easy, bloodless, grief-less, family-less killing in all the cowboy and gangster movies might have had anything at all to do with the beginning of the growth in today's overt violence in Western society.

Other movies were romantic, and often sheer fantasy. I could not by and large begrudge the ready-made fantasy component for all those in our Valleys whose lives were drab, harsh and unpromising, those whose imaginations had not been enlivened by schooling, and who day by day in the daily round suffered unremittingly 'the tyranny of the ordinary'. I think especially of many married women. In Garnant, single young women who were allowed to by their parents could at least dress up and go to the occasional dance in the green-painted, corrugated-iron Palais (de Danse). Some married women went there too, but socially that wasn't a proper place for a married woman to be. Most married women didn't work outside the home, and for most of the time were confined to housework and child-rearing in their own houses, with very few social leisure options. Men after all did leave home to go to work, they did have sports they could follow, night classes they could attend, pubs and men's clubs that many of them frequented, and for men involved in local industries, there was a heady, collective working-class sense at that time of being involved together in a progressive crusade for equality and justice.

Another of the cinema's possible effects was to enlarge people's expectations of life, and up to a point that too was good, of course. But even granting that, the movies probably went over the top in their total effect on people's dreams, obscuring for many who went to see them regularly the daily realities of their lives. The movies however have been a much, much bigger phenomenon than the effect on them either of any number of one-eyed practitioners, or of excessive fantasy or simplification. There were, after all, movies that entertained by telling great stories, and telling them superbly – *Mutiny on the Bounty*, *The Three Musketeers*, *Swiss Family Robinson*, *The Hunchback of Notre Dame*. Some of those were a plus from the viewpoint not only of entertainment but of artistic sensibility and integrity as well.

But in addition to explicit themes, many movies were predicated on values which, unless people chose and were able to regard movies critically, affected them subliminally. Most of the underlying motifs in movies I saw as a child went over my head of course. It was quite a few years later, when I began to read critical articles and books about past movies, that I discovered how much in them of great significance for better and for worse I had missed over the years.

Despite Sam Goldwyn's dictum that 'messages are for Western Union', there were movies with clear messages. Some of them, even when they had a blatantly chauvinistic element, were worthwhile, and many of the messages got through – about what democracy means, about the importance of the press, about how much one man who stands up can do. Such movies could inspire. The movie version of Somerset Maugham's *The Razor's Edge* had me walking around and behaving as Tyrone Power did in the movie for weeks on end. But even in those there were unspoken restraints. American movies for instance, while enthusiastic in their portrayals of one man bucking the system either at home or abroad, were always careful not to portray groups of men bucking the system.

There is now a small but significant Welsh – and Welsh-language – film industry, but back in those days movies did little or nothing for our own native Welsh-language culture, and not much for Anglo-Welsh culture either. Although there were movies made in England, they were swamped in numbers and in impression on us by Hollywood, so movies were a force which worked toward making us too a part of the great, homogeneous Americanised world. That world was certainly one we wanted to be introduced to, but its blessings were very mixed blessings. Balancing Jihad and McWorld remains a basic theme and challenge for our culture. However, there was one institutional bulwark that had some potential for counteracting any possible cultural and moral harm that the flood of 1930's Hollywood movies might inflict on us.

With the development locally of the secular society (first educationally, through the founding of a state-run primary school, then culturally, in the raising of the Workmen's Hall),

Christendom, a centuries-old European concept and reality which had been winding down for some time all over Europe was coming to its final and visible end in our village. Forces of change which had been straining at the bit for some time were at last decisively changing a largely theocratic community into a secular village. The chapels, which up until then had been the prevailing culture, were beginning to be called upon to be what hardly any form of Western Christianity had been for many centuries: a counterculture. Unready or unwilling to recognise the nature, depth and permanence of the change, they were consequently unable to accept it and adjust to it; unable to face the fact that the new order of things was a call for a new self-appraisal of their role in their community.

I can't remember any formal antipathy in the chapel to the cinema, but there were parents who didn't allow their children to go except when accompanied by them, and even then only if the movie were specifically for young people, or something of the order of a Shakespearean classic, or an expression of a high-minded or religious theme. Neither can I imagine any of the local ministers standing in line in the cinema foyer to buy a ticket. In fact, I don't believe I ever saw any of the local schoolteachers doing that. That was partly perhaps the response of people brought up in a community whose dominant influence up till then had been the oral culture of the chapel, and who were biased in favour of the supremacy of the spoken word, and against a medium which was predominantly visual. For such people there was always also a high degree of moral ambiguity about movies, and the titles of some of the movies did nothing at all, to put it mildly, to remove their doubts, particularly in reference to women. They ranged from the titillating to the suggestive – *Ladies Love Brutes*, *Tarnished Lady*, *She Couldn't Say No*.

All in all though, it must have been a frustrating time of transition for church leaders. Their lives were so totally invested in the world of the chapel, and up until then they had experienced nothing but a high tide, but they now sensed, saw and feared the tide turning against them. The cinema, by bringing some of the change into stark focus, must have seemed to them a catalyst (if not the catalyst) for the reversal of their own fortunes, and the fortunes of their religious communities.

Although effectively the war had been lost, what some chapel leaders did was to fight rearguard battles tooth and nail. In my valley, frustration eventually boiled over into a 'holy war' on the issue of rehearsals held in the Workmen's Hall on a Sunday evening (after the chapel services had ended) by the local operatic society. The local press, and even the British press, avidly picked up on the matter and put it in the full glare of publicity. Church leaders felt they were doing something they vaguely thought of as 'witnessing', but the whole could only be a storm in a teacup – the die was already cast. Nevertheless, knowingly or not, the chapels were now the counter-culture; and for better or worse, the only one in town.

CHAPTER 6

The Chapel

'THANK GOD WE are a religious people', says the Revd Eli Jenkins in Dylan Thomas' *Under Milk Wood*. Religion for me, in the Wales of my childhood, was 'chapel'. The word 'chapel' wasn't just a description of a building used for worship, it was also used to denote one of the only two religious orientations available in most Welsh communities then. To discover to which of the two orientations a person had allegiance, one simply asked, 'Church or chapel?', and even many of those who didn't attend either were absolutely clear about which one they didn't attend. But the question itself spoke of a great historical divide in Welsh religious life.

For us chapelgoers then, 'church' meant two things. It meant the Anglican Church, the established episcopal Church which resulted from the separation of the Church in England and Wales from the Roman Catholic Church during the reign of Henry VIII in the sixteenth century. It also meant the actual building where Anglicans worshipped – from the outside a cruciform building, usually surrounded by a cemetery, often approached through a lychgate, with bell tower and stained-glass windows; and on the inside a floor of flagstones or tiles, a baptismal font near the door, a prayer stool and kneeling hassocks in each pew, at the front a lectern and a pulpit (each to one side), and an altar against the centre of the back wall. It was also named after a saint. To those of us who weren't 'church', it was a building in which up-and-down worship (possibly with poor congregational singing) was conducted according to a book, and led by a man called the Vicar, who wore a surplice during worship and a dog-collar everywhere else at all times, possibly wasn't much of a public speaker (and wasn't expected to be by chapel people), and who, even after the Anglican Church in Wales had been disestablished in 1920, still considered it implicit in the very meaning of his job that he had a duty of care, in principle if not in practice, for all the souls in the parish.

As a child however, I was hardly aware of Anglicans, for I belonged to the mainstream of religious life in Wales then, of which Anglicans were no part. Mainstream religion in almost all of Wales at that time was the religion of the Welsh-language Nonconformist denominations – Baptists, Congregationalists, Calvinistic Methodists (Presbyterians now), and in lesser numbers, Wesleyan Methodists (Methodists now), and Unitarians. All of these were essentially breakaways, in one way and another, and at different times, from the established Anglican Church of that time.

Chapel meant the kind of building where these Nonconformists worshipped. They were mostly square or oblong boxes, usually plain as could be on both the outside and the inside, with clear or opaque windows, oftener than not with a gallery running around three sides on the inside, and perhaps surrounded by a cemetery.

Chapels correspond to nothing that preceded them historically. They are in no way representational or symbolic; they convey no sense of mystery and are not intended to. Essentially they are functional buildings – they are preaching stations. The seating is arranged around a central pulpit so that people can sit, see the preacher, listen to the reading from the Bible, follow the extempore prayer, but above all attend to the sermon, all delivered from the one pulpit by the minister. Usually too, chapels have been named after some Biblical place – Hebron, Jerusalem, Carmel, Nazareth, Bethlehem. The principal of a Welsh University College, son of the minister of a chapel, wrote in his autobiography that walking to school every morning for him in Aberystwyth, a town on the west coast of Wales which had very many chapels, was like taking a stroll through the Middle East.

The couple of churches which served Cwm Aman had been built in out of the way places on the other side of the river from the main road, but the chapels – certainly the larger chapels, guardians of the gospel, morality and propriety – were all on the main road, and in conspicuous places close to the centre of the village. 'The chapel' – Bethel Newydd in particular – was the other institution that was a part of my young life.

There were five workdays, then there was Saturday, and there was Sunday. Although it held various kinds of meetings on weeknights – fellowship meetings, prayer meetings, choir practices, meetings of the cultural society – the chapel seemed to accept, albeit grudgingly at times, the fact that it was other things that most of its members would be doing at those times. It felt, however, that it had a moral right to claim Sunday, the Lord's Day, for itself – all of it, and from all of its members – and it did. Two worship services were held each Sunday, one in the morning and one in the evening, and on Sunday afternoon there was Sunday School. Around those gatherings, there would probably also be a committee meeting of some kind for some people, or a choir rehearsal, or some chore to carry out. If chapel members didn't attend a service on a Sunday, they would be expected not to do much of anything else on Sunday either, certainly not in public, nor would they therefore feel free to do so – 'the Nonconformist conscience' cast its net wide.

Members were encouraged to attend both Sunday worship services, were told that they ought to, and many did, although the format and aim of both services was essentially the same. But at that time, the evening service was the pre-eminent service, the one which most members attended. Sometimes a minister, wishing to chide those who didn't attend the morning service, would facetiously refer to them as black pads, a colloquial name for a species of cockroach which came out only at night.

There were good reasons why those who worshipped once

only on Sunday should make that service the evening service. Conceivably some spent Sunday morning recovering from a late Saturday night, and some women stayed home on a Sunday morning to prepare the grand midday meal. But there were also those for whom one service per Sunday seemed quite enough (as well as those for whom that was more than enough!). These too tended to choose the evening service. For those with an interest in singing, there might be the attraction of a choir practice after the evening service. With no need to hurry home to be in time for midday dinner as after the morning service, and to be in time to attend Sunday School in the afternoon, there would also be more opportunity following the evening service to socialise, especially for young people. With people pressed for time, as he too was up to a point in the morning service, the evening service was the one for which the minister would have prepared his longer, grander and perhaps better sermon – or at least the one he considered to be his better sermon. That in turn became another reason for those who chose to attend only one service on a Sunday to make it the evening service.

I think that perhaps my parents fell into the black pad

Bethel Newydd Chapel (photo c.1911)

category of chapelgoers when I was a child, since most of my memories of my attendance at chapel at that time are of sitting – often sleeping – next to them at the evening service. I remember that it was after being awoken by the hymn following the sermon one Sunday night that I first revealed what was to become a lifelong questioning approach to religion. I asked my mother why it was that I could keep awake for two and a half hours watching movies in the Workmen's Hall on a Saturday night, while I couldn't stay awake even for the length of a sermon in chapel on a Sunday night! I might have still been a little sleepy even as I asked my question, since I can't remember whether Mam replied.

The format of both Sunday services at our chapel was simple, and there was little deviation from that format. Basically it consisted of a sung intrada, a hymn, a reading from the Bible, a hymn, an extempore prayer by the minister followed by a congregational recitation of the Lord's Prayer, the announcements and the offering, another hymn, a sermon, a final hymn, the minister's benediction, and a sung benediction. A Welsh chapel service has been described, not entirely inappropriately, as a hymn sandwich.

However, not all the fillings in the sandwich were of equal value. The moment for which everyone in the service waited, the moment for which all else tended to be regarded as the prelude, the great moment, was the moment after the third hymn when the minister got up to preach his sermon. This tended to downgrade the readings from the Bible and the prayers, and sometimes a preacher would declaim against that tendency. Nevertheless, for most chapel ministers, their premier title in their own eyes as well as in the eyes of others was not shepherd, or worship or spiritual leader – and certainly not, God forbid, priest – but preacher. It was not for his administrative skills nor usually even because of his pastoral care and dedication that he had been invited to be the minister of his congregation, or would be invited perhaps some day to minister to a larger congregation, but for his reputation as a preacher. Indeed, when he moved, it might be said that he had been called not to another chapel or flock, but to another pulpit.

The minister at Bethel Newydd when I was a child was a handsome, erudite and good man, and I liked him very much. Yet sometimes the Baptist minister from Glanamman would preach at Bethel Newydd, and although I was aware even then that our Mr Leyshon was the more able man, I preferred to hear the Baptist minister from Glanamman preach than Mr Leyshon. That was for one reason and one reason only. Some Welsh preachers of that time, during the peroration at the end which some of them thought intrinsic to a fine sermon, would break into a *hwyl*. This is an untranslatable word used to describe a droning, sing-song mode of delivery that was presumably intended somehow to intensify the message. How it originated and what evidence there was for that effect, I don't know, although one may come across the phenomenon in, for instance, the black church in America. There was certainly a measure of *hwyl* in the speeches and sermons of Martin Luther King. The Baptist minister from Glanamman spoke throughout his sermon in the same tone of voice and with the same inflections as he would in conversation, but Mr Leyshon often broke into a *hwyl* as he came to the end of his sermon. I didn't mind visiting preachers doing that so much, but as a child it always embarrassed me deeply, and made me cringe inside, when our own Mr Leyshon went into such an unnatural mode of delivery among us, his own people – whom he would later, as we exited through the front door, greet and address quite naturally as if nothing untoward had happened. I used to wonder at times whether the grown-ups felt as I did or whether my feelings were peculiar to children – or perhaps peculiar to me – but I never asked anyone. I wonder now too, in retrospect, whether my response had any link at all to the fear a child is said to have when one of its parents is even a little inebriated.

Most preachers followed a format as fixed as the service itself in the composition of the sermon. A Biblical text, an introduction to deal with any textual problems and to explain the context, three points to draw out the message, and the peroration at the end. Some with a mind for mnemonics strove to find three points beginning with the same letter, as in God's power, God's patience, and God's pity – not a bad teaching aid where many amongst the congregation had not received much formal education.

There were different kinds of preachers. Some were in the pulpit to save individual souls, others argued for social justice; some were scholarly, others were poetic; and some did their best to present their congregations with a balanced diet by attempting to do it all over time. Some too were actor-preachers who could deliver tremendous sermons with magnificent self-assurance. It used to be a commonplace to say that Welshmen such as Richard Burton and Anthony Hopkins, who went into the theatre as actors and in time became household names as movie stars, would have become great preachers in former days in Wales, when the professional stage wasn't an optional outlet for their talent. Richard Burton himself wondered as much in more than one television interview.

Some of the pulpits were stage-like, with ample room in them to move, and some of the preachers would use them as a stage. The most polished and artistic sermon I have ever heard was preached by a stocky minister with one weak eye that led him to hold his head a little to one side, and who allowed the hair at the back of his mostly bald head to grow long, in what was generally regarded in those days as a poetic hairstyle. Raised on a farm on the west coast of Wales, as a young man (like many other young men in that area of Wales) he had become a sailor – actually rounding Cape Horn on a sailing ship. But eventually he left the sea to become a preacher, and in addition to being worldly-wise and clever, he had also over the years not only made of himself a very literate person, but had become a remarkably fine poet too.

Among other high points in that sermon, he told the story of Zacchaeus, the short tax collector from Jericho who climbed a sycamore tree to see Jesus when he walked by, and to whom Jesus announced that he would call at his house that day for a meal. Simon B, as this preacher was known to his colleagues, created a scene in which Zacchaeus returned to his home to tell his wife that this celebrated visitor to town was coming to their house 'for tea', and he acted it all out, using his own words. Without mentioning Zacchaeus' height, or lack of it, he took Zacchaeus' part on one side of the pulpit, making him look upward as he addressed his wife, then he shuffled almost imperceptibly to the other side of the pulpit to give her response, which he gave looking downward a little. As a congregation, we who listened to Simon B that day were mesmerised by the total subtle hour-long performance. Sermons shouldn't be longer than ten minutes in this sound-bite era, according to some of today's pundits. Perhaps they should add, 'unless, that is, you can make it seem like ten minutes.'

Twice a year in almost every chapel there would be a preaching festival, to which a well-known preacher or two, probably from distant parts of Wales, would be invited as guest preacher(s) for the festival. Some of those festivals were held on weekdays, but should they be held on a weekend, as was usual in the Valleys, the afternoon Sunday School would be replaced by a preaching service, and there would be a service on Saturday evening as well. Ministers and members of other chapels, including those from chapels belonging to other denominations, could then come to the Saturday evening and Sunday afternoon services, and enjoy listening to the pulpit giants of other traditions.

It's difficult to overestimate the place of preaching and preachers in Welsh life at one time. For many people it was a great fascination, and the great preachers were princes. I once read an account of the building of a new chapel toward the end of the nineteenth century. The opening was celebrated on a weekday, a Thursday, with four services, at six and ten in the morning, at two in the afternoon, and at six in the evening. There were three sermons by three different preachers in each service, and not one of the preachers – each of whom came from quite a distance (in Welsh terms) – preached twice that day. Twelve different sermons and twelve different preachers in one chapel on one day! Nor did a sermon come to an end after the minister had said 'Amen', or the congregation had left the chapel. Later in the day it would be discussed in the home, and at work the next day a coal miner who was a regular chapelgoer would in all likelihood be asked by a regular chapelgoer from another chapel what the texts of his minister's sermons had been the previous day. The first coal miner would reciprocate the question, an informed discussion on the various contents would probably follow, and others might join in.

Once a month, in Bethel Newydd, the morning service would be a children's service, during which the sermon would take the form of a children's address. At this service, one child would take a Biblical reading, another would read a prayer, and others would announce the hymns, reciting all the stanzas from beginning to end perhaps. At one point in the service most if not all the children would go to the front of the chapel, turn to face the congregation, and recite a verse or verses from the Bible. Some, at home with the ethos of such a situation, would recite whole passages from memory without breaking a sweat, while others, for whom such services can't have been much fun, would hang their heads, mumbling incoherently and with great discomfort, or hurriedly reading a few words from a scrap of paper they were trying to conceal in their hands.

But if the primary responsibility of a worshipper in a chapel was to sit down and listen, his or her secondary responsibility was to stand up and sing. The singing was usually to the accompaniment of an organ, and in the case of the larger chapels, very fine pipe organs, often with the console and organist – and many organ pipes – in full view behind the pulpit. At one time it was not uncommon even for small orchestras to play a part in the regular services of some chapels.

Everyone who attended chapel had been taught from childhood a system of music notation called sol-fa, so that with the use of hymn books in which tunes were printed in sol-fa above the words, even members of the chapel with no understanding of music otherwise could sing their part by sight. As the whole congregation was, in effect, the church choir, congregational hymn-singing would be in four parts.

The Welsh language, which can conjugate its verbs and therefore doesn't need all the ancillary words that English verbs use, can be very compact at times. 'I will go' can be expressed in Welsh by the two-letter word, *af*. Such conciseness enabled those who wrote hymns in Welsh to get a great weight of meaning into one line. The authors of hymns in Welsh were very often also skilful poets in their own right outside the world of hymn writing, and the themes of Welsh-language hymns, like the themes of negro spirituals, were always mighty, powerful themes. The result was the production of many hymns of great strength and distinction. Powerful tunes were needed to ensure that hymns of that texture didn't sag. There were composers who rose to the challenge so magnificently that in the event the tunes could stand on their own without the words which had inspired them, with the result that hymn tunes have been one of little Wales' most enduring exports, as hymn books all around the world will confirm.

The chapels had originally closed their doors to art in all its forms, eschewing paintings, stained-glass windows and decorative stonework – and for a period even organs – but in time art sneaked back in again, through the back door as it were. This was done not only through the craft of sermon-making, through sermons which were sometimes literary and rhetorical masterpieces, but through hymn composition and congregational four-part singing of such power and beauty that they could at least compare favourably with such phenomena anywhere else in the world. An attempt may be made to separate religion and art, and for a time it can have a degree of success, but it seems that religion and art can't be permanently divorced.

Singing, like preaching, had its high celebration. Once a

year in most if not all chapels, a *Gymanfa Ganu* – a hymn-singing festival – would be held, usually on a Sunday but often on some public holiday such as Easter Monday. Ahead of time, a committee would be appointed to choose children's hymns for the morning service, meditative adult hymns for a quiet, sleepy afternoon service, and for the evening service – apart from a quiet hymn or two for contrast and to give hard-working voices and perspiring conductors a break – full-blooded hymns, beginning with calculated restraint perhaps, but working up to great, fiery crescendos. All of the hymns would be printed – words and music (mostly sol-fa, but also musical notation copies for the *oligoi*) – along with the names of the guest conductor for the day, the local precentor and organist, the president of each session, and the committee, in a special programme for that year.

To be chosen to serve on a *Gymanfa Ganu* committee was heavy duty indeed, since not only did you get to propose hymns and vote on them – and there were also choruses and anthems to select – you got to take flak as well, if for some reason the *Gymanfa* wasn't the resounding success some people thought it had been the previous year when they were on the committee! The committee was also responsible for choosing and inviting the guest conductor for the day of the *Gymanfa*.

Apart from the music itself, these conductors were the most ecumenical feature of Welsh chapel life at that time. Many of them were soloists in their own right, or piano teachers, or conductors or accompanists of some local choir, or precentors or organists at another chapel, and some of them were all of the above! Some were flamboyant, kept their hair long, wore bow ties, had stage names, and advertised their availability in the denominational press. Often without formal education in music or in anything else, many of them brought themselves to a high level of musical competence, studying at home for this or that diploma – most of which seemed to be referred to by at least four letters, for instance ARCM (Associate of the Royal College of Music). The owner of the diploma would be entitled to use the letters after his name, and would usually want to (theirs was a very competitive trade). Not infrequently he would have three such diplomas, which would mean an alphabet of letters after his name on a *gymanfa* programme. A few guest conductors would be women, while some were chapel products who had become lecturers or even professors of music at colleges and universities.

The local precentor would for weeks beforehand prepare those who were ready to attend rehearsals, and then the guest conductor, after conducting the final rehearsal, would conduct the *gymanfa* on the great day. There would be two groups of singers. There were those who sat downstairs: visitors, people who couldn't sing (or didn't want to), and elderly people. These would be asked to stand and sing the occasional hymn, so that they got to stretch their legs, and so that their clothes wouldn't get permanently stuck to the varnish on the pews if it were a humid day, but no more than that was expected of them. Then there were those who sat in the balcony upstairs: a kind of unofficial choir, arranged in four parts, and consisting of those who had faithfully attended rehearsals. These were expected to stand for the singing of every hymn, and much was expected of them. A *Gymanfa Ganu* would be an orgy of hymn-singing.

The children's service at a *Gymanfa* would be yet another occasion for the children of the chapel to be on display. Some of the better public performers would here again be invited to read from the Bible at the beginning of the service, or to read a prayer. Each stanza of every hymn would also have been allocated ahead of time to some child to recite aloud, and during that service the conductor would now and then ask questions of all of them. The children would sit in the balcony, close to the conductor, sometimes boys on one side and girls on the other, and the conductor could easily use them to humour and please the congregation. Should one particular child emerge as precocious, or even simply foolhardy, the conductor knew he or she had a straight man and was home and dry!

Most chapels of any size also had a choir led by the precentor of the chapel, which would present concerts at which they would perform such oratorios as *Elijah* or *Messiah* or *Judas Macabeas*. Well-known soloists would be engaged, some of them well-known names in Wales, but some of them perhaps from London. In the chapels of Wales in those days, great numbers of people without much in the way of formal education were not only acquainted with some of the best singers in Britain and with music by some of the Western world's greatest composers, but could themselves recite, word perfect from beginning to end, the texts of great, majestic works.

Music, however, could also be an Achilles heel for a chapel. The cause might be a clash of personalities, the preacher not sympathetic to the musical programme perhaps, and the precentor or the organist (sometimes the same person) possibly a prima donna. Sometimes, however, it had to do with the nature of the beast. Everyone who wanted to sing in the choir simply didn't have the voice to be accommodated, and not even the best soprano the choir had ever had, even if she were the chapel secretary's wife, could sit in the front row during a public concert once her tremolo had passed a certain point of no return. Artistic standards and religious inclusivity don't always coincide. So music could be a cause of dissension often enough for a phrase in Welsh meaning 'the devil of singing' to become a common idiom.

Religious education was traditionally important for chapel life, and the main instrument was the Sunday School, which was held on Sunday afternoon. This was for adults as well as children; the adults in scattered corners of the chapel, and children usually in the vestry. In that the original Welsh Sunday Schools had taught an illiterate peasantry to read in order that they should be able to read the Bible, and that the ability to read had led to a desire to read books other than the Bible as well, the Sunday School has played a significant part in the development of education in general in Wales. In my childhood, although the Sunday School movement had changed in many ways, it was still a very powerful educational institution. It was a place where adults, male and female, would be led by a teacher in discussions and in studies of Biblical passages, following a chosen syllabus for which some minister-scholar would have prepared a special commentary that was printed in the denominational weekly newspaper. Sometimes a book was especially commissioned and printed to serve classes that studied that year's Biblical syllabus.

The teachers were often wise and mature people who prepared for their task diligently, and the discussions ranged from the meanings of particular Biblical passages, through age-old topics as great as free will and human destiny, to issues of the day. It was also a place where children were told great Biblical stories and given moral guidance, and where young people were given an opportunity to air their doubts and flex their mental muscles in arguments – usually then to do with science versus religion – with their long-suffering teachers.

Whereas the churches in my valley when I was a child were quite anglicised, the chapels, despite an ambiguity at the time in the attitude of many social and chapel leaders to Welsh and Welshness, were in practice a bastion for things Welsh. The Anglican Church had produced some outstanding Welsh-speaking Anglicans in the history of Wales, but the people served by the church I knew locally were people the chapels didn't aim to serve – gentlefolk; monoglot immigrant English speakers; English immigrants who had learned Welsh but were more comfortable in English; Welsh-speaking immigrants to the area who had a family tradition of Anglicanism; Welsh-speaking locals who for reasons of upward mobility tried to be English; and some locals who were Welsh, Welsh-speaking Anglicans, and happy to combine in their persons all three. The chapels were for Welsh speakers; they conducted their affairs entirely through the Welsh language. Although some preachers spoke in an affected, esoteric, highfalutin, pedantic Welsh, at best the worship service from beginning to end was conducted in a Welsh that was flexible, strong and a standard for all. English-language chapels were few and far between in the Valleys generally, and never seemed quite able to take off even in places where it seemed as if they ought to. It was often implied by Welsh worshippers that religion and the English language didn't really go together – at least not in Wales!

The chapel also promoted Welsh culture in general. Almost every chapel held an annual competitive cultural festival called an eisteddfod – an untranslatable word, which described an event that was common outside the chapels too. It would include reciting poetry, literary competitions, solo, group and choral singing, instrumental playing, and much more, and for all ages. Judges from outside the membership of the chapel would adjudicate, and for the children there would be prizes: sums of money given in small multi-coloured bags attached to long ribbons, which were made in advance by a team of women and would be presented to children to hang around their necks should they come first, second or third in one of the competitions. It was at an eisteddfod in some chapel or other that many Welsh people who went on to become well-known names in the entertainment industry first stood up alone before an audience and performed publicly.

Then there were the fun times: the parties and the Sunday School trips. In those days of home-cooking, with hardly any women working outside the home, the parties were feasts. There were Christmas parties and Whitsun parties and summer parties. A certain amount of unacknowledged competition got into this sphere too, since some women had village-wide reputations either for cooking in general or for their version of some particular delicacy.

The Sunday School trips I can remember were all to Swansea Bay, 20 miles away. We left our homes early in the morning, five or six hundred souls perhaps, and we all converged on the short, steep hill leading down to the railway station from the main road. Mothers would be holding their children's hands tightly; fathers and older children carrying picnic baskets, bags containing towels and bathing suits, and carriers containing changes of children's clothes in preparation for the possibility that they would fall into the sea before they donned their bathing suits, plus umbrellas and rain coats – in case. Then we waited in large groups on the station platform for the train which was to take us. Every child who had attended Sunday School four times during the preceding 12 months travelled free – Sunday School attendance soared in the weeks preceding the annual trip!

Keeping a host of excited children in sight and out of mischief in such an intriguing environment as a railway station platform, then keeping them away from the edge of the platform when the train drew into the station, was a mammoth task. It was always a safe bet that one or two small boys would be in the station toilet when the train was about to pull out, either due to the call of nature or pure mischief – who knows. The train would be a 'special', which meant that all the coaches would be reserved for our chapel alone and the train wouldn't stop to pick any one else up at any station along the way, it sped onwards until it had arrived at its final destination. While the train was in motion, boys (although told a hundred times not to) insisted on sticking their heads out of the windows and got cinders in their eyes from the smoke of the steam engine.

Our final destination was a station called Swansea Bay, actually on Swansea Bay. You stepped out of the train onto a sand-covered platform and the beach was right there before you. You could take your shoes off on the platform and be walking on the beach within ten yards of the train. And for some it was the one day in the year when they saw the sea.

Those Sunday School trips, or 'excursions', were revelatory times for us children. Younger deacons that for the rest of the year seemed – because they were – stiff in dress and movement, and whose normal conversation with us seemed to be composed entirely of Thou-shalt-nots, released for that one day from the burden of role-playing, became young, innocent and carefree. They would play cricket with us, yelling like small boys when someone was caught out, and touch-rugby, throwing themselves around, falling flat on their faces and tussling with us on the sands. Some of them would even change into bathing trunks and come into the water with us, and most of the others would at least roll up their trouser legs and paddle in the sea. Mothers and grandmothers who normally wore voluminous clothes so we small boys had no idea that they had thighs like other people, on the beach exposed what seemed to us vast expanses of marble-white flesh, which bemused and intrigued us as we ran by them. Sometimes we would throw or hit a ball near to one of them to give us an excuse – while pretending not to notice – to take a closer look.

There would always be one panic, such as someone losing a child, before the long day's end. I was that child one year. At the railway station, I needed to answer the call of nature, and my mother took me to the ladies' toilet – a heavy, cavernous structure, as all railway buildings were in those days. She left ajar the door of the cubicle I was to use, and told me to join the rest of the family back on the station platform when I was done. I, however, closed the door, an immense self-locking door whose catch was too high for a child to reach. When I was ready to leave and realised what I had done, I shouted and bawled, but there was no one else in the toilet, and the sounds of trains arriving at and leaving the station not only drove me into a panic but ensured that no one outside could hear me. When I didn't appear after a while, my mother, not dreaming that I could still be in the toilet, had everyone around her scouring the platform for me, and it was finally another woman entering the toilet who rescued me and returned me to my proper owners. But the journey homeward on the train was always a quiet one, with children irritable but tired, mothers with faces like tomatoes and watchful lest anyone should inadvertently lay a hand on their burning shoulders, and fathers happy as sandboys after a day of reliving their childhood.

The chapel was a patriarchal world. In theory, women could preach and a few did, but that was a rarity, and when it happened that fact was more of a talking point than the content of the sermon. Although in a chapel such as ours –

Bethel Newydd, a Congregational chapel – the power lay with a gathered meeting of all the members, that kind of meeting was in fact unusual. It was more likely to be held because the deacons needed authority from the congregation to take some course of action they were already set on than to solicit their views. In practice the powers that be even in a Congregational chapel were ostensibly the deacons, and they too were virtually exclusively men. I say ostensibly because all knew that in the case of some deacons at least – and everyone knew which ones – their minds on any question in life were made up for them by their wives!

Deacons then were chosen usually when they were at least middle-aged, and they were chosen for life. Underneath the pulpit was a curved raised pew where they sat during a service, and in which they turned around to stand facing the congregation when hymns were sung. The original aim of facing the congregation was so that they could exercise pastoral oversight – see who was there, and who wasn't, so the minister could be informed. But few people now remember that function, and facing the congregation today is only a way for deacons to see who doesn't have a hymn book out there so that one can be taken to them. There's a story that an American once visited a service in a Welsh chapel, and on being asked later what he thought of the service, said he thought it a good service as far as he could tell, but that he couldn't say much in praise of the 'choir'! But being a deacon, especially in a large, powerful church, was a status in the community and could reflect on a deacon's family as well as on him.

Like many other things in this world, chapels carried within them an ambiguity. If on the one hand they were congregations gathered around core beliefs and values which produced a huge outburst of energy, life and uplift, on the other they took upon themselves (and perhaps had to, since no one else was taking it on) the role of being the community's moral policeman. The minister and the chapel were great moral forces in the community. The influx of people from other communities to serve the needs of industry in the Valleys, many of them young and rootless, and the harsh economic and working conditions of their lives had once led to much heavy drinking. With the drinking came debts and violence, including family violence. One of the greater triumphs of the chapels and their ministers had been their considerable success in setting a tone for community life, in bringing their communities to a remarkably high level of civility. They did so largely by defining, according to their lights, the good life. The definition they proffered and encouraged could be demanding and inhibiting, but it was essentially a good way for that time and place.

Like the Biblical faith of the Jews, their definition of the good life went into great detail. Sunday in particular, which they often surprisingly referred to as the Sabbath, was a focus for many of those details. On Sunday all the pubs in Wales were legally closed. Originally the law which enacted that ordinance – a law brought about due partly at least to the influence of the ministers and the chapels, and peculiar to Wales – had been intended as a protection, on at least one day of the week, for women in the new industrial conglomerations of the Valleys whose husbands drank and abused them every other day of the week. No unnecessary work was to be done on a Sunday either. As a child I was even forbidden to whistle anywhere, including in the house, on a Sunday, and certainly to play in the street. I remember how confused Mam was one year when Christmas Day fell on a Sunday and I wanted to go out to play with my new gun and bow and arrows. The final adjudication, I remember, was a compromise: I could play on the street with my new bat and ball, but not the new gun or bow and arrows!

But Sunday had its pluses too. Sunday midday 'dinner' was the greatest meal of the week, with meat, an array of vegetables (in summer and autumn fresh from the garden) all covered with a wonderful gravy, followed by a bowl of sweet rice, and washed down with a glass of pop. Afternoon tea was also special on a Sunday: bread (home-baked of course, sliced thinner than usual and richly spread with farm butter), pears, peaches or apricots from a tin, covered with cream, plus a variety of cakes – sponge cakes, angel cakes, and cakes peculiar to Wales such as a yeast loaf cake with currants we knew as *bara brith*, and *pice bach* or Welsh cakes – small, flat, rounded currant cakes baked on a griddle.

Above all perhaps, even if it did involve busyness from morning to night for those who attended every church activity on Sunday, and even if it involved work for Sunday School teachers, chapel officials who stayed behind after the evening service to count the offering and balance the books, and women who prepared, set and cleared the meals at home, Sunday was simply a very different day. It was a change from the other days of the week, a change of patterns and activities, but a change too of emphases and priorities. Even at the mundane level of a change being as good as a rest, Sunday was, by and large, for most of the community – even, I suspect, for many of those who wished it were otherwise – a good day, or at least a day that was good for them.

All codes of morality can become external, and there was much that was external about chapel morality. The Welsh writer Caradog Evans, who wrote critically in English about Welsh country life and was therefore never forgiven by many of his fellow Welsh speakers for exposing our failings to the outside world, translated *Y Parchedig* not as 'The Reverend', but as 'The Respected'!

Chapels and their ministers were not always blind to the ambiguities of some of their stances. Chapel cultural societies sometimes held debates on issues such as whether it was more sinful to read on a Sunday a newspaper written on a Saturday, or to read on a Monday one written on a Sunday. The matter would not be discussed without great humour, but not without a serious underlying awareness of life's unavoidable complexities either.

The system, like all such systems, produced some inevitable hypocrisy too. The respectable chapel official who now and then called into the pub for a drink, but used the back door and a back room. The senior rich, powerful deacon whose daughter, despite needing a very voluminous white dress, was allowed to get married in the chapel, while daughters of less prominent members, though needing dresses a little less voluminous, weren't. One picked up some of the flavour of such things even as a child.

The chapel, in practice if not in intent, in its heyday offered a spectrum of options, not all strictly religious, through any of which people could engage with the chapel. To some, no doubt, it was only an interesting meeting place: somewhere to socialise, particularly on a Sunday evening. Families were large, houses often small, television was a long way off, there was nowhere else to go on a Sunday evening, and chapel was the place to be if you wanted to belong and be seen to belong to the prevailing social as well as religious milieu. Good attendances, uplifting music and participatory singing, sermons often well delivered, artistic, dramatic, informative and insightful, made it not the worst place in the world to be either. People of my generation who were exposed as children to chapel life, even those whose interest in chapel life didn't run very deep and who sooner or later turned their backs on it all, might leave with an inhibition or two – sin and guilt were a very big deal in most chapels – but they couldn't possibly leave without also having gained much else from their early dealings with a chapel.

Some perhaps would have acquired a husband or a wife through some chapel or post-chapel activity. On a Sunday night, there was nowhere but a chapel service where young men and women could go on a regular basis, dressed up in their finery, and be able to see each other in formal glory. On summer evenings, after the service, a crowd of young people from Bethel Newydd would stroll in their Sunday best up the open, tree-lined and almost car-free valley road to Gwaun-Cae-Gurwen, the next village up, while the young people who had been to chapels in that village would walk down toward our village, Garnant. Winks would be given, a stop for polite flirting might follow, and occasionally a couple would break away from their respective groups and walk together, apart from the others. Many marriages originated on Sunday night jaunts along that road.

Many would surely leave chapel life with some appreciation of, and an abiding respect for, all words spoken and written, but particularly for rhetoric. The chapels helped create within their own life, and in the life of the community at large, a verbal ethos which not only became a launching pad for many a young poet, actor or politician, but which also fashioned appreciative if not always discriminating audiences for those who took those options, as they began their journey.

They would all leave also knowing many at least of the Biblical stories which underlie Western culture, and which have given both the Welsh and English languages, explicitly and implicitly, many of their images and metaphors and similes – the wisdom of Solomon, the patience of Job, the salt of the earth, washing one's hands of something.

Nor could anyone who had attended chapel as a child or young person have possibly failed to pick up a store of hymns. One can play golf with another Welshman who might not be able to recall, if asked, when he last went to chapel, apart from the occasion of a funeral, but he starts whistling or humming quietly as he walks from tee to green and one suddenly realises that without being conscious of it himself, it's a hymn tune that he's whistling. Although the various denominations in Wales in the past chose to produce their own separate hymn books, enough of the better hymns were held in common that at a critical moment in an international rugby match in Cardiff between Wales and England – or Scotland, or Ireland – if someone in the crowd starts singing a hymn, thousands of the Welsh supporters will pick it up (some singing the melody, others the bass and tenor parts), and soon it will seem to the opposition as if they are not only playing against 15 Welshmen but also struggling against heavenly hosts.

Sometimes it goes deeper, much, much deeper, as I learned myself vividly one night. I was sitting alone at my father's bedside, and he was dying. His eyelids opened briefly now and then. That almost certainly didn't signify even flickerings of consciousness; but I wasn't absolutely sure, and he loved hymns, so in case those occasional momentary openings of his eyes meant even fractions of seconds of consciousness, I wanted him to go from this life to the next to the accompaniment of hymns that he loved. I began quietly to sing hymns, many of which had been a part of my own consciousness from my earliest days, and I continued to sing without exhausting my repertoire until he stopped breathing and grief overtook me. I fell to my knees with a sobbing that shook and racked my body for a long time. After that outpouring I never shed another tear. Looking back later, with a renewed awareness of the capacity of powerful hymns to penetrate one's defences, I was not only amazed that not a single hymn that had come to my mind had been inappropriate, I was also astonished at the number of hymns I had been able to sing, word for word, from beginning to end.

For children and young people in particular, chapels and their ministers, possibly above all else they did for them, offered them heroes who embodied values and ideals not on offer in the surrounding culture. Our cricket and rugby idols, which we boys might want to acknowledge enthusiastically among our peers, were not necessarily giants of the spirit, any more than most of the heroes offered to us on the silver screen were top-drawer heroes. Through the chapel we heard of alternative heroes, to keep silent about among our contemporaries perhaps, but to cherish in our hearts if we were so moved.

There were Biblical heroes: Moses, Samson, David, Peter, Paul. There were Welsh religious heroes: our sixth-century patron saint, David, who adjured people to do the little things in life, and Mary Jones, a young girl whose efforts to secure a Welsh Bible for herself inspired a minister, Thomas Charles, to form the first ever Bible Society. There were pioneers of our own brand of churchmanship, such as – a personal hero of mine – the Oxbridge-educated John Penry, hung in 1593 by the

British religious establishment at 30 years of age for his efforts to secure a Bible in Welsh so that his countrymen, monoglot Welsh most of them, might read it for themselves.

There were great Welsh missionaries and the stirring stories of their accomplishments, some of them against the greatest odds imaginable: John Williams in the South Seas, Griffith John in China, David Jones in Madagascar. And there were other great Christian names, further afield ecclesiastically and nationally: William Wilberforce, the Englishman who fought against slavery; Father Damien, the Belgian who worked with lepers, even after he himself became a leper; Mary Slessor of Calabar in Nigeria, the Scottish millworker who learned the native language and became a magistrate and diplomatic emissary there; Albert Schweitzer of Alsace, who had doctorates in four separate disciplines, but dedicated his life to serving the sick in Lambaréné in West Africa; Toyohiko Kagawa from Japan, a convert who worked in Kobe's slums, became an adviser to Japan's post-war cabinet, and toured Europe after World War II to apologise for Japan's atrocities in the war. Scattered among the names of the Christian great and good were also names of people who were simply very remarkable human beings: Mahatma Gandhi, the Indian who practised Satyagraha (soul force, or non-violent protest); and Marie Curie, from Poland, who with her husband developed the theory of radioactivity and discovered radium and polonium, experimenting on herself. Mr Leyshon spoke to us about such people at children's services, we were told about them in Sunday School, and when a gift was given to each child who had reached a certain age at Christmas parties, it would be books about such people that we were given.

Talk about Jesus was a constant in chapel life of course, with the words delivered and received in various degrees of intensity. For those young people who wished to 'follow Jesus' more closely than others wanted to, there were two avenues. For young women, there was nursing; and for young men there was the ministry. Though of course some young women went into nursing for other reasons, many young women consciously took up nursing, even though they might not admit as much, out of a sense of Christian vocation; and at one time no less than ten of Bethel Newydd's young men were in training to become ministers.

That world was soon to come to an end. As a child, I had a consciousness of World War I since there was hardly a house without a large, framed photograph on the wall of a man in uniform. Sometimes this was of someone who had survived the war, the man of the house perhaps, but sometimes it would be a photograph of a father, husband or son who had not survived. But I was too young to have any awareness of the gathering clouds of World War II, too young to realise that already blowing steadily and strongly was a wind of change which was to become a hurricane. Men would go away to the armed forces, and women too would go away, to the armed forces, to work in ordnance factories, or to work on the land. Many for whom their faith, unknown to them perhaps, had been too entwined with a culture which was now changing, a faith which had finally perhaps deteriorated to become just a residual attachment to a building, would gain confidence from fresh experiences, from encounters with other models of living, and return home to a new world of greater diversity and fewer restraints, a world in which it was easy now to detach from what they saw as merely the religion of the chapel.

Churches in America boomed after World War II, so a minister there could hardly fail to be a success in the fifties. However, in Europe generally, and therefore in Wales, institutional religion went into freefall. Today most of the chapels in Wales, most without benefit of regular ministers, are kept and attended by a handful, often principally of elderly women. But to me as a child, the world of the chapel seemed to be a stable and unchangeable world.

I'm aware now that there must have been other kinds of people in our valley, including people who lived full, good, useful and happy lives without personal benefit of chapel, but those people didn't belong to my little world then. The people who belonged to my world and certainly those whose influence on me was greatest were people who, without being overly pious, had a genuine respect for the chapel, kept in touch with the chapel, steered clear of the chapel's excesses, but took from it its better insights, and reflected the glow of those insights in their daily lives. And one of those was my Tad-cu.

CHAPTER 7

Tad-cu

I SOMETIMES WONDER how it feels to be able to trace one's ancestors backward for generation after generation, to live in an ancestral home in which the walls are galleries showing portraits of past bearers of one's family name, mortals in whose faces one can recognise one's own eyes or chin or turn of the head; some whose solitary distinction is that their portrait was once painted, but some with dark secrets, and some illustrious. Owning such a lineage ought to add a dimension to one's identity, and enhance one's confidence and poise.

I have a hazy recollection of being led when I was a child to stand before the oldest ancestor of whom I know, one of my great-grandfathers on my mother's side. Unfortunately I have no recollection of his face now and I know nothing of him except where he lies buried, that he fathered seven sons and one daughter, and that one of those sons was my maternal grandfather, my Tad-cu, in whom I have invested all my personal experience of ancestry.

In one respect whose consequences can't possibly be exaggerated, Tad-cu and Mam-gu and their contemporaries were a unique generation. They were among the last representatives of a stage in the story of human life that extended backwards as far as its very origins: they still lived at a time when dependable family-planning aids were not yet available anywhere in the world. Certainly none of Tad-cu and Mam-gu's children, grandchildren or great-grandchildren have raised families anywhere as large as the one Tad-cu and Mam-gu raised. With some variations, we all essentially belong to the 2.4-children-per-family generations.

The beginning of the availability of such aids in the West marked an unprecedented turning point in the story of homo sapiens. It's difficult for us who live today in societies this side of the change, unless we have been constrained in the enjoyment of its many benefits (through religious disapproval for instance), to imagine what life must have been like before the change. The extent of the change, in women's freedom and health, in privacy and intimacy, in sexual mores, in domestic chores, in parenting, in home finances – and sometimes in keeping children alive, just keeping them alive – means it may be absolutely impossible for future generations to imagine what it must have been like then.

One of life's features in Tad-cu and Mam-gu's time, then, was that many women, if not most women, continued to give birth until nature brought her childbearing years to an end. When my sister was born, Tad-cu and Mam-gu were also parents of their own two-year-old child. Large families born over many years were the norm at that time, not the exception.

As did most large working-class families in the Valleys and elsewhere in those days, so too did Tad-cu and Mam-gu know about hardship, including what must have been for most the fiercest hardship of all, the death of a child. One year, early in their marriage, Tad-cu and Mam-gu in the same week lost two children, who died of unrelated illnesses which would almost certainly not have led to their deaths today. One was a three-year-old son, who died on a Tuesday; the other was a year-old daughter, who died on the Thursday.

At that time it was a custom at the funeral of a small child for the father of the child to carry the coffin himself some part of the way. The children that Tad-cu and Mam-gu lost, Thomas John and Marion, were buried together on a Saturday, and Tad-cu carried each of their coffins in turn in the funeral procession that wended its way up the hillside to Hen Bethel. That poignant fact has become for me a powerful image of hardship in what we sometimes glibly call 'the good old days'. But dealing together with what life threw at them made of Tad-cu and Mam-gu a powerful team. Yet I always thought of their home, and still speak of it, as Tad-cu's house.

Mam-gu was a remarkable person. She always wore the kind of dark clothes that her community considered appropriate to a woman of her age, and her greying hair – even though she lived to a good age it never went completely white – was drawn back tightly and tied at the back in a bun. She was small, slim and very agile. One of her party tricks was to bend forward from the waist, legs together and her back absolutely straight, put both her hands completely and flatly on the floor, and challenge her grandchildren to do the same. It was something my sister and I were never able to do, however. Although my sister could at least touch the floor with the tips of her fingers, I have never been able to do even that without bending my knees.

Mam-gu was a storehouse of nonsense sayings which she used to fob off my sister and me when we asked too many questions of her as she went about her endless chores: 'What's this, Mam-gu?' 'Oh, that's something without salt that I use to salt pots and pans.' (it makes better nonsense in Welsh!) or 'Where shall I keep this, Mam-gu?' 'Well, why don't you keep it where squirrels keep their nuts?' She was also a feisty character. Mam has often said that in Tad-cu and Mam-gu's marriage, Mam-gu was really the driving force. I had never thought that until I heard Mam say so, but perhaps she was right. Marriages are frequently mysteries to those on the inside, let alone to those on the outside.

But society was more patriarchal then than it is now. Although Mam-gu of course made many of the decisions to do with the day-to-day details of running the house and raising the children, when larger issues arose affecting the whole family, it was Tad-cu who was expected to articulate the view that would prevail. When such situations arose, he would want Mam-gu's input and would listen readily to anything any one of their children might want to say – from the oldest to the youngest – and having heard them, he would try and take a long-term view of what he judged was best for all. Mam-gu and their

Mam-gu and Tad-cu

children, after having had an opportunity to say their piece, would always defer to that view. That his view would be more of a 'sense of the meeting' view than an autocratic decree must have made deferring to it easier than it might otherwise have been, especially for the more argumentative among his offspring. A confident but undemanding person, Tad-cu carried the authority with which he was entrusted by the whole family with a modest gravitas.

That authority was symbolised to some extent at mealtimes. Meals were eaten at the large rectangular table in the centre of the living room. Tad-cu always sat in the same chair, an armchair situated between the table and the fire and which normally faced the fire, but which was turned around and moved forward a little toward the side of the table when it was time to eat. Although he didn't actually sit at the head of the table, his chair was the only armchair at the table, so that in an oblique sense he presided over meals. Should he for some reason not be there for the meal, no one else would dream of sitting in his chair – unless one of the children did so momentarily out of mischief.

He did not have very many requirements of his children, and the ones he did have seem to me to have been simply helpful, even if not absolutely necessary, to the smooth running of a large household. One of those was that the children were not to talk at the table during mealtimes, and another was that no one was to leave the table until their plate had been cleared. I too was subject to those rules when I ate at Tad-cu's house, and even now when I don't finish a meal served me on a plane, I half expect a flight attendant to come along and tell me that I won't be allowed to disembark until I have cleared my plate!

Sensing early that it was with him that ultimate influence rested in my little world, my childhood memories don't revolve around Mam-gu, as they mostly don't revolve around Mam. Besides, Tad-cu and Dad were the ones who wore the kinds of clothes I looked forward to wearing one day, who did the kinds of things I assumed I would do when I too became a man, who spoke about kinds of matters that were already beginning to interest me, and whose gestures I began to imitate from a very early age. It was they also who consciously accepted most of the ultimate responsibility for shaping my growth.

The grandfather-grandson relationship is by its nature a very protected one, free from so much that might be troublesome in other relationships. It's free from the strains and stresses of specific, practical expectations and responsibilities attached to parenting. Since it's an overlap of both of the extremes of the parabola of life, when there isn't much to know about the life of one, and when that one hasn't the capacity yet for grasping much of all there is to know about the life of the other, it's free from the possible complexities of information overload – each knowing too much about the other. It's also a relaxed relationship where neither party is at the height of his energies and powers, and so both are free from personal ambition or a drive toward a competitive goal. It's a relationship free too from the possible staleness and constraints of a long history.

What with earning a living, family matters generally, parenting in particular, taking care of the house and the garden, and a hundred and one other chores, Tad-cu in fact wasn't able to spend a very great deal of time with me during my earlier years, but he was never so consumed by other matters that when he did spend time with me he was ever brusque with me. He was always gentle and patient, and very protective of me, his first grandson. Firm and decisive in his dealings with his own children (the youngest of whom was only four years older than me), 'Don't be hard on the boy' was a frequent cajoling refrain of his when I was disciplined by either of my parents in his presence.

Despite the little time that he was actually able to spend with me, Tad-cu was a great and benign presence in my universe, a presence that from time to time enriched my world immeasurably by a wonderful instinct he had for the penetrating and memorable gesture. I'm speaking of a gesture in the sense of something that didn't have to be done and which wouldn't have been missed at all if it hadn't been done, something that was totally unexpected, and which was, more than anything else, a statement.

When I was seven, Tad-cu called me to his side one day, took me out to his garden and led me by the hand, slowly, very deliberately, almost ceremoniously, to one of his apple trees. It was a tree close to the house, the smallest tree of all in his orchard – but it was fruitful, and the apples were eating apples. He stood quietly in front of it with me for a moment or two, then said to me, 'You see this tree? From today onward, this tree is yours. I am giving it to you. You will own all the apples that grow on this tree every year now, always they will be yours, and yours alone, to do with just as you choose, and I will make sure that everyone else in the family understands that.' So in one fell swoop he made me even richer than my schoolteacher aunt – his daughter – had made me when she gave me that collection of show-marbles. I was now not only the richest boy in my class, but in the school – perhaps in the whole, wide world! What was it to own a cricket bat and wickets and a cork ball, and to eat strawberry jam every day – every meal! – compared to being the sole proprietor of a complete, real apple tree? What other boy could possibly match, let alone beat that boast tomorrow and tomorrow and tomorrow? 'I've got a penknife.' 'Have you? Do you know what I've got? I've got...' or even, 'Let's go and steal some apples from Will John's garden – one of his apple trees is right next to the road, and the apples are almost ripe.' 'You go. I don't need to steal apples, I've got an apple tree of my own.' Wow!

Another time, much of my body had for some months been covered with a very irritating skin rash which at the end of every day became inflamed and kept me, and so my parents too, awake much of the night. No amount of suggestions and ointments given us by our own local doctor had done any good at all. One Saturday, Mam and Dad together were intending to take me by train to Llanelli, a town some 16 miles away, to see the owner of a chemist's shop there who had acquired a reputation for being able to cure skin ailments with a home-made prescription. Mam and Dad had got me ready to go early that morning, but while they were still getting themselves ready, there was a knock on the door and in came Tad-cu, dressed in his Sunday best. He announced simply, 'I'd like to take the boy to Llanelli today if that's fine with you.' Mam and Dad made mild protestations to do with him not needing to do that and so on, but they ultimately deferred to him of course. To have him take me by the hand and lead me out of the house, to walk at his side through the village and down to the railway station, to sit next to him on the train, to walk with him at the other end from the station to the chemist's shop, to have him be the one to reassure me while the chemist who owned the shop examined me, to have him be the one who discussed my condition with that man, to eat lunch with him in a café in that strange town, and to do so much of it all again coming back – to have Tad-cu to myself for all that momentous day, was a treat more awesome than not having to go to school for a month of Sundays, and for one whole day it made my skin rash worthwhile!

I was fortunate enough to have my grandfather physically present in my life for a long time. I was 23 years old when he died. When I recently spoke about him to his next grandson, hoping to exchange reminiscences, he reminded me that he was only 11 when Tad-cu died, that he had always lived some way from Tad-cu's house, and so has only a few, vague recollections of the man who was his Tad-cu too. I became newly aware of how blessed I have been to have Tad-cu's enriching presence for so long in my past, and still he continues in my memory as one of the 'tender mercies' of my present.

Tad-cu was a coal miner, and he looked as you might imagine a man who worked underground should look. If men were born to be coal miners, they should be born with his physical characteristics – a square face, a strong jaw, a thick neck, broad shoulders, deep chest, and a low centre of gravity due to short but sturdy legs. 'I'm not small', a man of Tad-cu's build (and mine) once told me, 'in fact, I'm a comparatively big man, I wear a large size in hats and collars and shirts and jackets – I just have short leg bones'. Tad-cu might have said the same. Over the years he had also, of course, like all who earned their living at a coalface, acquired the telltale blue scars of the coal miner – small cuts suffered underground, which had congealed before the coal dust in them could be cleaned out. He had some on his face – one or two on his chin and cheeks, a conspicuous one across the bridge of his nose, and several on his forehead. He also had many on his hands and forearms, and some too no doubt on his back and chest and legs.

He was a man, and the son of a man – who might also, as far as I know, have been the son of another man, etc. – whose genes were dominant. I once saw a picture of a brass band from the village where Tad-cu was raised, which showed four of his six brothers as they were in their twenties. Although I had not known any of them when they were young, picking them out was like picking out grapes from a bowl of nuts. If those four, plus his two other brothers I suspect, plus Tad-cu, Tad-cu's three sons, and his five daughters for that matter, his eight grandsons and seven granddaughters could all be put side by side at the same age, no one would doubt for a single second that we were all related! The first time I saw my older daughter, the eve of the day she was born, when the bone structure of her head could be clearly seen, what struck me forcibly was how like Tad-cu and his children and his children's children my firstborn was also.

Tad-cu had a good reputation as a coal miner and took great pride in that. In those days before machine mining, before cutters and grabs and conveyor belts, an experienced miner would often be put to work standing up before his own stall at a coalface. Perhaps a shotman would have fired a small explosive or two before he began his day's work, to loosen the coal for him, a young lad (possibly his son, learning the craft) might be with him to help keep the stall clear by dragging rubble away on a large wooden tray to which a length of rope was attached, and the miner would work away with pick and shovel to fill a tram standing on rails nearby with coal. Once the tram was full, the miner would write his initials on it with a piece of chalk that he always carried in a waistcoat pocket. The tram would then be pushed by the man and boy – or perhaps be hauled away by a pit pony – to a large lift-cage if the mine were a pit (that is, entered by a vertical shaft), and the tram would be carried up to the surface with other trams in the lift-cage. If the mine were a drift (that is, entered by a downward slope going into a mountainside), the tram would be pushed or hauled to where it could be hitched to other trams, and they would all be pulled together up the incline to the surface by a cable wound around a large drum in an engine-house on the top. At the surface the trams would be shunted to a siding where there was a weighbridge. There, a checkweigher would estimate how much of what was in each tram was coal and how much was slag, and the miner whose initials were on the side of that tram would be credited for the coal. Some miners would deliberately slip some slag into the bottom of their tram, hoping it wouldn't be noticed. Others, simply lazy or careless, shovelled coal and slag indiscriminately into the tram, letting the checkweigher work out how much they should be credited for. That was less work for the miner of course, but more work for the checkweigher. I have been told on good authority that whenever the checkweigher at the Raven Colliery, where

Tad-cu worked, saw Tad-cu's initials on the side of a tram, he would always without further ado credit him with a full load of coal.

During difficult times locally or nationally in the coal industry, when there was no work due to a strike, a lockout or a recession, Tad-cu, who knew where small coal seams were to be found not too far from the surface, could and would himself open a small outcrop mine up on the mountainside. With the aid of his sons and Dad, and perhaps another man or two, he would dig a vertical shaft, not much wider than the width necessary to enable one man, standing in a bucket hooked to the end of a cable, to be winched down it by another man. But he it was who would supervise the initial dig and the ongoing work, which would only begin when the shaft was finished and pronounced safe by him.

There would be no room for more than one man to go down such a shaft and work the coal in the seam at any one time. That man would cut coal, fill the bucket with it, tug the line, and the men at the top would wind up the bucket. There was no ventilation at the bottom of the shaft, and so after a man had worked down there for a while, the air would become very warm, which could cause the man working there to become lethargic and possibly therefore careless. When he felt it was necessary to come to the surface for fresh air, he would give a signal on the rope, he would be hauled up, and one of the other men would take his place. However, if he were down for too long a time in Tad-cu's opinion, Tad-cu would require him to come up whether the man thought he needed to or not.

Tad-cu it was too who would be ultimately responsible, as the face of the seam being worked was moved forward, for any propping up of the roof that was necessary to ensure everyone's safety there. At the end of a day's work the men would take it in turns to wheel the coal down the mountainside in barrows to the homes of one or more of them. The whole operation, though small, could be a dangerous business, calling for a range of knowledge, various skills and good judgement, but

Tad-cu had all those in abundance, and those working with him trusted him implicitly.

Tad-cu was something of a pioneer in the community. His house was large for a coal miner in that place at that time. He had simply decided one day that the small house he lived in then wasn't an adequate dwelling space for a large family to live in with dignity, so he borrowed £350 from an aunt of his, and had a house built at a cost of £350. That was a great deal of money there in those days, but I suspect that all the transactions were actually made with cash. His aunt was probably quite a number of years older than him, and her generation in the valley would be very, very unlikely to have entrusted any money to a bank. To most of them a bank would be an intimidating place socially, a financial club to which only business people and rich people should belong. The comparatively wealthy interior of the bank itself too would make it somehow suspect to ordinary valley people then. They certainly would seldom, if ever, be in a position where a cheque book might be useful. Their likely preference would be to stash any money they had saved in the house somewhere – behind an unused fireplace, under a mattress – and a little of it, for easy access, under a stair-carpet.

He named the house Bron-y-Clydwr, after the home of Hugh Owen, an Oxford-educated Puritan minister, who was one of Wales' seventeenth-century religious leaders. Why he should have done that I don't know, just as I don't actually know how he would even have known about Hugh Owen, but I'm moved that he did.

Although his first four children had names that weren't Welsh – Thomas John, Mary Hannah, Marion, and Dorothy, and his last two were named Anne and Eira (the latter is a Welsh name meaning 'snow', and is often given to a girl born when there is snow falling or on the ground, but it's not forcefully Welsh either in sound or significance), the other four were given names that couldn't be more Welsh – Cranogwen, Meurig, Moelwyn and Caradog, names rooted in the history and in the land of Wales. I wish I knew what lay behind his very Welsh period, for he was then unquestionably swimming against the linguistic current of the day. And why, if there were a reason at all, the drift back again away from such assertively Welsh names?

In a place and at a time when so many houses were attached to another house or houses, partly because such houses were cheaper to build, the house that Tad-cu built was detached, and whereas most houses in the Valleys then were 'single-fronted', Tad-cu built a 'double-fronted' house – that is, the front entrance stood in the centre of the front of the house, and had a window on each side, the windows of the two ground-floor front rooms.

At the back, on the ground floor, there was a fine large kitchen-come-living room on one side and a sizable pantry on the other side, and beyond that a bathroom. Of the two ground-floor rooms at the front, one was simply called 'the middle room'. It had a bookcase, a dresser, a sofa under the window, fireside chairs, and a table always covered with a warm, wine-coloured, heavy, chenille cloth bordered with tassels. This room wasn't

Bron-y-Clydwr

used much, but it had a soft pile carpet, and was always heated (free coal was part of a miner's wages) by that closed brown stove which had panes of transparent mica at the front. It was the room where I did so much of my early reading.

The other front room, the parlour, I never saw used at all. It was small, and cold even in the summer, with lino covering the floor. There was against its outside wall an empty, ornate, tiled fireplace in which, I suspect, a fire had never been lit. In the window, an earthenware pot containing an aspidistra was enclosed in a large, decorated glazed vase which sat on a tall, narrow stand, and in the centre of the room stood a round, heavy, one-legged table bearing two large thick books, one on top of the other. The larger one underneath was a big Welsh Bible with thick, black covers and two brass clasps. Inside, it was prefaced by pages on which family information was to be entered, and had been, and still was when I was a child. The other book was a family photograph album, also big, with not only all the places for photographs filled on each page, but enclosing as well a great number of other loosely-inserted snapshots which bulged the covers to bursting. There was in many houses locally at that time a similar room, which in fact would only be used when someone died and there was need for a cool room in the house in which to lay an open coffin. Upstairs there was a landing and four good bedrooms, all almost equal in size. All the front rooms of the house had, in addition to curtains, heavy venetian blinds with wooden slats, which were never completely raised.

Tad-cu had had the house built on its own in a field. At the time it was constructed, it was reached from the main road by a footpath, but by the time I was born it stood on a road to which and from which other roads came and went. Very few things went wrong unexpectedly in Tad-cu's house, since he always maintained it in good condition. That meant such regular chores as cleaning roof troughs, checking drainpipes, changing a cord on a sash window when it first began to appear frayed, burning off old paint on windows and doors and giving them two new coats, both an undercoat and a topcoat. Prevention is better than cure was another mantra I could have learned in Tad-cu's house. But in addition to maintaining the house always in prime condition, Tad-cu was also constantly making improvements in and around the house – a paved patio area at the back, an outside WC, a cement path through the garden, the large coal shed. He was a man able and ready to turn his hand to many things.

After his house had been built and other houses had been built around it, Tad-cu, continuing the pioneer strain in him, was the first in the street to install a fixed bath with running hot water. Later still he was the first to own a 'wireless set'. The wireless was in two parts: a receiver and a speaker. The receiver was a plain, light brown, varnished rectangular wooden box with a very small central window in front, through which you could see part of a vertical white dial with black numbers on it separated by gradation marks. On the right there was a large knob which, when you turned it, moved the numbers in the small window up or down to get the right station. A similar knob on the left controlled the volume. The speaker, which rested on top of the receiver, was made out of shiny, very dark brown – almost black – bakelite, with gothic-shaped apertures at the front through which the sound emanated, the apertures covered with pale gold-shot cloth. It wasn't a wireless that was ever used to provide anything so aimless as background music. Merely looking for something being broadcast which might be interesting was frowned upon by Tad-cu. This wireless was never used unless whoever wished to listen to it knew beforehand what he or she was going to listen to, and when that programme had finished, he or she turned it off.

When I was a child I was astonished late one night to see several men being ushered into Tad-cu's house just as I was being ushered out to go home to bed. That memory returned and puzzled me many times over the years, but it never came to mind when my parents were at hand. When it finally did and I asked them about it, we worked out together that it must have been the night in 1937 when every male in Wales who didn't own a wireless set, and many females too, must have been cosying up to someone who did. It was the night the Welsh coal miner, Tommy Farr from Tonypandy in the Rhondda Valley, fought Joe Louis at the Yankee Stadium in New York City for the heavyweight championship of the world. Tommy Farr was beaten, but only on points, one of very few opponents not to have been knocked out by the US's Brown Bomber.

Sometimes I would stay in Tad-cu's house overnight, and if it were summertime and I had had to go to bed before it was quite dark, I would sit on the low windowsill in the front bedroom in which I usually slept when I was there, striving to keep awake until the gas lighter came, so that I could look down and watch his nightly ritual around the lamp in front of the house. He would come riding a bicycle on which a small ladder was hooked. He would prop his bike against one side of the gas lamp, unhook the ladder from the bike, and prop that against the other side of the lamp. The top of the ladder would rest on two arms, reaching out under the lantern above, and just wide enough to receive the ladder. The gas lighter would then climb the ladder, open the glass door on one side of the lantern, reach inside, turn on a gas tap there, a pilot light inside would ignite the gas, and the mantle would become aglow. The gas lighter would wait a moment to make sure all was well, then close the lantern door, descend the ladder, hook it back onto his bike, mount the bike, and ride on to the next lamp, leaving a world lit now not by the dying sun but by a small, friendly incandescence. The light thrown out made a halo against the night, drew to it a few moths, illuminated a circular area of the pavement below, and then I went to bed satisfied, as if the whole process had needed my supervision to ensure it was done properly.

Once or twice, when other visitors too were staying at Bron-y-Clydwr, I slept with Mam's three brothers in the large bed in the back bedroom which they shared together. The three usually slept side by side, but when I joined them, the older brother and I would sleep at one end of the bed, the other two at the other end. There was much tickling of feet and cavorting before everyone finally fell asleep, and there was some accidental kicking of each other throughout the night. Then the morning would begin fresh and early by whoever first awoke starting a pillow fight.

Such shenanigans apart, Tad-cu's house was for me a haven of stability. A physical stability to begin with. It was a plain, well-built, strong house: It had an inner stability to it as well, epitomised by the clock which hung on the wall facing the back door through which you entered the living room from the back of the house. It was a large clock, with a casing below that had a glass front through which you could see the swing of the pendulum inside. It had a face that would win no prizes for design today, since it was coloured a light brown (a lot of the Welsh world was coloured with various shades of brown in those days), not very much lighter than the Roman numerals on it, and the hands were so embellished that you had to look very hard to discover which was the big and which the little hand. But what I remember most about that clock is its tick. It was a slow tick, a background sound you never became fully conscious of until late on a lazy, warm Saturday or Sunday evening in the summer perhaps, when almost everyone was out. Now that I'm much older I couldn't stand the tick of a clock measuring my hours away, but it spoke to me then of the regular tempo of life at Tad-cu's house. Tad-cu too was a dependable and methodical person. He would wind the clock regularly, and check its time against the fob watch attached to a chain that he carried, as so many miners did in those days, in his waistcoat pocket. I don't recall that clock ever stopping while he was still alive.

Behind the house there was a wooden shed in which Tad-cu had at one time kept and bred canaries. He had even competed with them in bird shows, but by the time I was born he had finished with that hobby. The shed was by then a toolshed, in which, as he used to say, there was a place for everything, and everything had its place. Proud and protective though he was of his tools, he didn't mind if I, even as a child, took one down and used it or played with it – as long as I took only one at a time, didn't use it for any purpose for which it was clearly not intended, and put it back in exactly the right place! And he was very much aware that in laying down those ground rules he was transmitting values as well as taking care of his own personal world.

Then there was Tad-cu's garden. At the very top there were the remains of a stone pigsty. Tad-cu Glanamman still kept pigs in the sty at the top of his garden. My rare visits to Tad-cu Glanamman's house were always tiresome for me, partly because we went there by bus, which meant I had to wear nice clothes, and partly because while I was there I was constantly being told not to get my clothes dirty. That was very confining for a small, busy boy. Within that parameter I couldn't wander to find other boys I might be able to play with, for they would be wearing their play clothes and would probably be engaged in some activity that would make a mess of my nice clothes. About all I could do that had any interest for me would be to wander alone up the garden, climb to the top of the wall around the sty, sit on top of it, feet dangling inside the pen, do some pig-watching, and hope my clothes didn't get dirty. Sometimes there would be one pig in the sty, sometimes two. Sometimes they would be inside, in the sty itself, in which case I would try and imitate pig sounds in an attempt to get them out, but sometimes they would already be outside, in the run. Food left over in the house, and some stuff from the garden too, went to feed the pigs – potato peelings, stale bread, windfall apples, cakes grown mouldy.

The pig was a big part of the household economy of many miners' homes. It was usually bought from a farmer as a piglet – one day my father-in-law, a steel worker, bought a piglet from a farmer and carried it home under his coat on a bus! Then it would be fattened, and when it was fully grown a local butcher would be hired to come along and do the killing in the yard behind the house. The squeals of the pig would be heard streets away, and its blood would be channelled down a drain at the back of the house. Then the carcass would be laid across a bench and boiling water poured over it so that the skin could be scraped clean of hair. Next, the carcass would be cut up, and portions of the better parts of the pig would be given as gifts to family and friends. Sides would be salted and hung up on hooks from the kitchen ceiling, to provide readily available bacon slices for cold, winter mornings. The pig's head would be boiled, chopped and moulded into a dish called brawn, and the liver, chopped and seasoned, would be baked into meatballs called faggots. Very, very little went to waste. Even the pig's bladder might be given to boys who asked for it, and who would blow it up and use it as a football!

I was at Tad-cu Glanamman's house twice when a killing took place, and twice was more than enough for this small boy, so I didn't regard my other Tad-cu's house as being a disappointment for not having a sty still in use at the top of the garden, or lacking in action for not having an annual slaughter or two any more.

Even without such drama, life at Tad-cu's house seemed to me much more interesting than life at ours. There were more people actually living there, of course, and partly for that reason there were more callers there too. But in addition, something exciting was forever going on there. A load of coal would be delivered perhaps. It would usually arrive without any more warning than 'probably some time next week'. It would be hauled on a horse-drawn cart. The front of the cart could be tipped up, the back of it opened, and then the load would slowly slip down. The coal would be dumped onto the road outside the coal shed behind the house. The coal shed, built of stone, was spacious and low. It had a concrete floor, and was topped with a corrugated iron roof. On one side, the side next to the road, there was a small wooden hatch which could be bolted on the inside. The coal would be passed through the hatch by the sons – very large lumps first, then successively smaller ones – and Tad-cu inside would stack them, fitting them together as snugly and securely as if he were building the Great Wall Of China.

When Tad-cu returned from work and found a load of coal had arrived that day, it would be all hands on deck. His sons had to cancel whatever arrangements they might have made to be anywhere else, in order to help, since whenever the load arrived, it was an aspect of neighbourliness to try to clear it from the road and the pavement before nightfall, even if it was raining. Were that to be completely out of the question for some reason, two or three storm lamps would be lit and placed around the load so that no one would fall over it in the dark and be hurt. Sometimes a farmer would deliver without prior warning an order of a cartload of horse manure for the garden, and that too would, if at all possible, have to be moved before nightfall – although in this case the concern, of course, was not so much that someone might fall over it, as fall into it. There was, of course, an abundance of well-embellished local stories about such happenings.

The coal delivered was the coal mined in our valley. It was the purest and cleanest of all coals. It looked like black marble and when it broke, it broke cleanly. You could rub a piece on your hand or wrap it up in a handkerchief and it would leave no mark. It burned slowly, becoming white hot, but with no smoke, and no flame except a small blue one, like the flame on a gas burner, dancing on the surface. A hearth fire built from anthracite coal would be allowed to burn low toward bedtime, when it would be almost smothered with small coals so that it would burn exceedingly slowly. The next morning, even though it might look completely dead, a little raking underneath it would revive it surely – but again, very, very slowly. An anthracite fire could, and by some would be, kept alive for a whole winter. Since it was very difficult to start an anthracite fire, everyone kept it going for a long time, letting it go out only if they felt it was desirable to give the grate a thorough cleaning. Some people kept a small supply of soft or steam coal at hand to start the fire again.

In those days the open fire was a very important part of life during the winter months, and much of a family's home life revolved around it. Before they were completely replaced, first by gas or electric fires, then by central heating, coal fireplaces became smaller, with low fancy grates in which only the top of the fire could be seen, so that the ash dropped quietly and invisibly into the ash pan below it. But the old-style grates were not only wide and deep, they were also comparatively high above the ground, so that when ash fell from them, it dropped visibly and audibly some 18" or more into the ash pan underneath, and needed attendance from time to time. Sometimes, should there be a substantial shift of the burning coal inside the fire itself, a considerable amount of white-hot embers might fall, not only through the bars below, but through the horizontal bars in front. Whoever was there at the time would need to check that none of it had fallen out onto the carpet in front of the fire, and perhaps prod the fire a few times with a poker to help it settle down firmly again. Sometimes it would be necessary to add some more coal. What with one thing and another then, an open coal fire in a high grate came close at times to seeming like a living creature, even a dependant that needed, as if it were a family pet, care and attention. It was a companionable presence, especially if you were alone, in a way a gas or electric fire, or even a low fancy grate, could never even approximate.

Like most other living-room fireplaces in the community, Tad-cu's fireplace had an iron plate at one side which could be pulled out to allow hot air to enter and surround and so warm a large oven there. But unlike most other fireplaces in the community, on the other side of the fire from the oven, Tad-cu's fireplace also had another iron plate which, when pulled out, heated a boiler of water, which supplied hot water to the kitchen sink and the bath.

In those pre-television days, it would be around the fire

that chairs would be arranged on a cold, winter's evening. Sometimes, if no one else were around, I would sit alone in front of the fire in Tad-cu's living room on a late winter afternoon, letting night fall without switching on the lights, just watching the fire, and hoping no one would come for a while and spoil the wonder of it all. If there were the tiniest hint of a draught, the white-hot coal would darken marginally, then lighten again, darken and lighten again, as if clouds were passing over it. If you sat close to the fire and kept looking at it, a strangely restful thing to do, you could see all sorts of shapes in the fiery furnace before you, caves and mountains, faces of people you knew, and if you were a small boy and adults had told you about it so that you were awake to the possibility, you could just make out the devil hiding in there. Should the fire shift even a little inside, there would be new shapes and faces, the devil would have disappeared temporarily and one would have to start looking for him all over again.

Even adults who were not close family played a major part in my early life, an experience that in practice so many children and young people are denied these days. Tad-cu's house is where I came across most of them at close quarters. Neighbours would call by, or distant family members from another village would come to pay their respects. Many of today's fashions and aids for looking younger weren't yet in vogue or available at that time, or certainly not in our valley, and so people who would not be considered very old now would look quite ancient then, and even more so of course as seen though the eyes of a child.

Visitors would sit around the fire and talk, exchanging information about other members of the family if they were relatives, and whether they were relatives or not, there would be talk about shared old friends. But there would be reminiscing too, about their particular communities, in the course of which an attentive little boy could pick up much about local history, and of the communal values shared by these people. Sometimes too views would be expressed about social issues and the politics of the day.

When I was taken to Tad-cu's house of an evening I would often sit quietly on a fender stool next to the fire, watch grown-ups enter, see them pull up a chair, and I would try not to make a sound, or even move at all, hoping that no one would notice me and realise it was well past my bedtime perhaps, so that I could stay late and listen to all that was said.

The conversation would always be in Welsh, but once, I remember, I completely forgot the need to be invisible in my eagerness to try out an English word I had just come across. I had read in a newspaper an advertisement for Ovaltine which included this word I had never before seen or heard, but whose meaning I thought I had been able to work out. It needed testing however, and the next time I was present and sitting on my fender stool perch when a group of adults were conversing in Tad-cu's house, I waited patiently for a substantial gap in the conversation, and when one came, I let out a long sigh, then piped up, 'Oh, I'm fatigued.' I don't remember being sent home and to bed as a result of suddenly making my presence felt in that way, but I remember that the pause which preceded the very loud outburst of laughter which eventually followed my interjection seemed to me a very long one.

By the end of his life Tad-cu was suffering badly from both arthritis and pneumoconiosis. The arthritis was the result of working long hours in wet conditions underground, and affected his whole body. I remember watching him at the table during a meal one day, tortuously trying to peel an orange with his stiff and twisted fingers. He tried in vain for a long time, refusing an offer of help from one of his children. Mam-gu, in her wisdom, knew better than to offer to help him – but finally the orange fell out of his hands, tipped the teacup in front of him, the hot tea spilled over his lap, seeped through his trousers, scalded his leg, and he cried out in pain, not even able to stand quickly or to hold the cloth of his trousers away from his skin, and I wished I were a hundred miles away so he wouldn't know I had witnessed his infirmity and his embarrassment.

Pneumoconiosis is a miner's disease, and nowhere was it a

greater danger than in the hard-coal section of the coal industry. The minute specks of coal hanging in the thin air underground were breathed in over many years by the miners. Trapped in the alveoli of their lungs, they clogged the microscopic spaces through which oxygen was passed into their bloodstream, rendering increasingly large areas of their lungs unfit to do their life-giving task so that in the end anything that took energy became breathless agony. In a coal-mining community in those days one would see men, some of them young men in the prime of their lives, shuffling along with a walking stick, trying to make their way as far as they dared from their homes, stopping every few yards to try to draw a few extra-deep wheezing breaths, without even enough energy to be able to respond to a friendly greeting from a passing acquaintance.

Tad-cu was a faithful chapelgoer, but he wasn't an overtly religious person. He wasn't, for instance, a man who would attend a weeknight chapel meeting and stand up there to speak about his faith or to lead the congregation in an extempore prayer - usually prerequisites for being considered potential deacon-material. He also had a quiet mind of his own and was never quite the conformist, which could also be something of a handicap in the deacon stakes. Despite the strong prevailing religious view that it was wrong to take a Sunday newspaper, for instance, he every Sunday received *Reynolds's Illustrated News*, a Labour party newspaper I have never either seen or heard of in any other context. But he never read it on a Sunday!

I was not surprised to learn when I was older that he had been active in trade-union work at the local colliery. Whatever views anyone may have of the pros and cons of trade unions today, there were few (if any) cons in those days. Edward Heath, when he was Conservative Prime Minister of the United Kingdom, spoke of 'the unacceptable face of capitalism'. There can hardly have been many places and periods when that face was more clearly unacceptable than in the coal industry in Wales in the twenties and thirties. For the coal miners, regular employment, safety measures, adequate health care, a fair wage, pithead facilities, and compensation for injuries and industrial diseases were all matters desperately calling for attention. To speak out, however, could be to invite discrimination. It took courage, and in view of everything else I know about him, I'm not surprised that Tad-cu often took his courage in his hands and spoke out for himself and for others. He was, in the eyes of the community at large, what most people would have described simply as 'a good man'.

Certainly he was the man who became Dad's model of manhood, the man Dad would have liked to have as his father, the man he adopted informally as his father. So Tad-cu affected me not only directly, through my personal contacts with him, but also indirectly, through the influence he had on Dad.

Dad admired many things about Tad-cu, but what he admired most of all about him perhaps – and which reflected his own upbringing – is that every one of Tad-cu's children was told by him that they could have as much education as they wanted and could handle, that Mam-gu and he would find money for that somehow. He opened the door of advancement as wide as he could to each one of them, and he had no favourites among his children – the ultimate accolade perhaps for Dad.

CHAPTER 8

Dad

IT IS OVER 40 years since he died. I have lost friends since, friends with whom I had long-lasting, firm, good, trustworthy friendships. But their deaths didn't hurt as much.

I was already 40 at the time and I still never expected to match him in many of the practical chores which were aspects for him of being a man – gardening, cementing a path, hanging a door, putting up a clothes line. For me, an important time during any visit he paid me after I had a home of my own was his tour of my garden. If he were to comment adversely on anything – 'The carrots don't look very promising', I would get very defensive – 'Yes, well, carrots don't seem to be at their best around here this year, Dad.' But any approval he expressed, 'That's a fine row of peas', was music to my ears. Over a year after his death I was looking at my garden one day and trying to understand why, much as I enjoyed gardening, I was letting it run to seed. It took me a while to realise that one of the reasons why I had been doing my garden up until then was in order to gain Dad's approval. He would not have wanted that power over me, even had he been able to comprehend it, but I was now going to have to find other reasons for gardening, and for some other things too, as it transpired. I think it was my last major step in becoming an adult.

Father is a resonant word, but it doesn't have the same resonance for everyone. I learned that conclusively one day, at a conference for men, in a retreat in Wisconsin in the USA. The conference began with a keynote address. In it the speaker, a softly-spoken man whose expertise and considerable experience lay in the area of the dynamics of family life, simply assumed matter-of-factly, without any hesitation, that many if not most of the men in front of him harboured a deep and long anger inside them because their fathers had been either physical or emotional absentees from their lives – or both – when they were boys. That seemed a preposterous assumption to me at the time – yet another instance, I was cynically sure, of what Europeans like to dismiss scathingly as American psychobabble. Yet when he had finished delivering his address, and the men there began to open up and unload in response to his lead, it soon became clear that not all men had been blessed with a father who was as constant and encouraging a presence in their lives as mine had been, and that for some of the men at the conference who were fathers, the prime motivation in their own parenting was a resolve that they themselves should do much, much better than repeat the pattern of parenting they had experienced at the hands of their fathers during their own childhood. Over the years since, understanding that has enabled me to make sense of the behaviour of many other men and fathers for whom articulating their experience with their own fathers would be out of the question.

A boy brings along with him into his relationship with his father his own distinctive person, plus both his general and his particular boyhood needs, expectations and hopes; but the relationship in the main is surely defined in most cases by the kind of person the adult in the relationship is, by who the father is, plus who he wants and tries to be.

C S Lewis, the Cambridge don and author, made a wry comment about his father on the very first page of his account of his personal spiritual odyssey, *Surprised By Joy*. He contrasts his Welsh father's emotional rollercoaster, Celtic temperament with the equanimity of his mother, who was English and 'went for happiness like an experienced traveller goes for the best seat on the train'. My father did not share this single-minded approach to happiness, and thought of it more as a consequence than a destination.

My father was, however, first and foremost a solemn man,

and this solemnity was also a family trait. He had a very solemn countenance, which was certainly a family attribute. To me as a child, the world his parents and siblings inhabited was a shadowy, twilight world. Their homes – his three sisters were married by the time I was born – had no variety or light or colour, no brightness, no flair, and all the memories I have of them are shaded a dry brown, as if my mind had photographed the furniture, upholstery, carpets, wallpaper and curtains all in sepia. Their conversations were no better – they had no flow, no spark of life. They were not 'bad people but their downcast attitudes offered not the slightest sign of redeeming uplift, their dull relationships no hint of flexibility or subtlety. I know now that they had no experience at all, no awareness whatsoever, not the slightest understanding, of humour, imagination, curiosity or ambition. Without drive or direction, they let life and its exigencies and conventions make all their decisions for them. They had imbibed from their society a certain amount of social capital – just about enough to keep them from falling below a certain level – but they themselves, apart from one sister, had no personal access to any reality, to any values or convictions or dreams, that might have enabled them to add one iota to that capital.

Their faces seemed to reflect the drabness of their confined inner world. When those faces were in repose their natural expression was a dismal, dispirited look, as if they personally carried the weight of the whole world on their shoulders, or had been burdened with a premonition of some great, impending disaster. Apart from Dad's brother Jim, who did sometimes give me a quick, fleeting smile, and even teased me at very rare moments – standing out from the rest of the family simply for that reason – and that one sister, Eunice, who wanted to be happy and in all fairness to her was always trying to be, the rest of them not only hardly ever smiled, their faces looked as if the bones, muscles and nerves in them hadn't been put together so as to enable them to operate the basic mechanics of a smile. I find it hard to imagine, and I don't believe, that any of them ever

Mam and Dad

laughed heartily, uproariously, collapsed into merriment, let alone pulled anyone else's leg even once in their lives, and should they even manage a wan smile at something said or done, it would have to be at something said or done by someone outside the family and not by any of them. Such a smile would have been a reluctant smile too, one forced from them as it were, and it would be accompanied by a wounded look in their eyes as if they had been pained by the process.

As I grew older I became more and more prone to tease Dad, and in doing so also became more and more adept at drawing a smile out of him, almost at will. That, in turn, became a pattern of relating to him. Over time that diminished my awareness of his solemnity, and sometimes I have had to be reminded of how solemn he was. My older daughter did that some time ago. I had been talking to her about Dad with great affection. Conscious of not being able to join in with me, and not wanting in any way to dissemble on a matter she knew was so important to me, she let me know very, very gently that she and her sister knew how much I loved him and looked up to him – 'But you see Dad, to us as children he came over as a very formidable person, and that's how we remember him.'

It's almost certainly not an accident at all therefore, that my very first memory of Dad is a memory of him exploding into helpless laughter – the only memory I have of him laughing until the tears came into his eyes. The occasion was an incident which happened in my first home, that flat in the house in Jolly Road in which I was born. I have vague impressions of some things that belonged to that home, but this is the only substantial memory I have of it. I am absolutely certain that I could not have been more than two years old at the time, since I know for a fact that I celebrated my third birthday in my second home.

On the day of the incident, Dad, as usual, would have returned home at the end of the day shift from the East Pit in Gwaun-Cae-Gurwen, the colliery where he then worked as an ostler, meaning that he took care of the pit ponies which were used underground to pull the trams. In his coal-dust-covered cap and working clothes, carrying his now-empty metal food box in his hand, an empty tea flask sticking out of the pocket of his jacket, his face and hands black from coal-dust, he would have caught a miners' bus from outside the colliery, which would have brought him the two miles or so to the bus stop opposite our police station in Garnant. Alighting from the bus and crossing the road, he would then have walked along the lane beside the police station which led to the footbridge over the railway line, crossed the bridge, then walked about 60 yards to the house, arriving at around three o'clock.

Just before Dad was due home, Mam would take the bath down from the wall of the shed outside, where it hung from a nail on a wooden beam. She would then give it its daily thorough dusting, carry it indoors, place it on the mat before the fire, pour into it cold water from a bucket, put a little bowl with a bar of soap and a cloth on it at its side, and see that a clean towel was warming in readiness before the fire. Then when Dad arrived, and while he was taking off his outer clothes just inside the back door, she would pour into the bath the water which had been heating for some time in a boiler on the built-up coal fire.

After he had stripped to the waist, Dad would kneel in front of the bath, test the heat of the water with his elbow, then wash the upper half of his body. Then he would sit in the bath to wash the lower half of his body. On this particular day, after washing the upper half of his body, he covered himself with a towel, took off the remainder of his clothes, and stepped into the bath. But he had left the bar of soap in the bath, couldn't see it because the lather generated already had turned the water to a milky colour, and as he stepped into the water he stepped also on the soap. He slipped, fell awkwardly and heavily, overturned the bath as he fell, and a bathful of soapy water surged over the floor. For a few seconds all was chaos. Mam's first concern was whether Dad had hurt himself, but as soon as she realised that he was alright, and that she was free therefore to focus on the mess all over the mat and the floor around, and on the hot water gone to waste, she sat down on a stool by the fireside, and wept. Dad, however, exploded into loud, uncontrollable laughter that lasted quite a while. Perhaps my memory has embellished some of the details for me over the years, but the event in essence was dramatic enough to have left a sure and a lasting impression even on the mind of a child not yet three years old. Added to that, of course; was the fact that Dad's reaction was so totally untypical of him. It pleases me greatly even now to remember his explosion of sustained laughter that day.

I'm always saddened, however, when anything reminds me of his solemnity. Whatever contributions his ethnicity or the chemistry of his family might have made to his solemnity, much of it had been imposed upon him from the outside, and eventually his solemnity saddened him too. Late in his life he confessed to me that he felt he should have enjoyed life a little more, smelled more flowers, and wished that he had. It's not that he wasn't able to enjoy himself at all, or that there weren't things that gave him great pleasure. As a young man he played rugby for a local youth team, and in the period when it was fashionable for even a young man to wear a watch and chain across his waistcoat, he sported a small medallion on his watch chain which showed that he had played for Grenig Rovers when they won some rugby competition or other. In his later years he enjoyed going to see an occasional rugby match, and reading accounts of rugby matches in the newspaper (especially if they were accounts of little Wales defeating England). Much later in life he would be thrilled to drive around proudly in his beloved small car, something he had at one time never dreamt for one second that he would ever possess. However, enjoying himself was an activity he only occasionally indulged in. It was something he would begin, continue for a while, then finish – after which he would return to being the solemn person he usually was.

But whereas his siblings were only solemn, Dad was also a genuinely serious person, who strove throughout his life never to compromise on his three early goals – of being a person of integrity, of doing something to improve the lot of his own family and his fellow workers and their families, and of trying to build a better world. It was an agenda challenging enough to make a very serious person of anyone!

One of the two things he was most serious about, serious to the point of passion, was learning. Although he had left school at 14 years of age – or perhaps because of that – he took advantage of any and all opportunities for improving himself. Most winters he attended a night-school class of some kind or another, laid on for coal miners, sometimes specifically for unemployed coal miners. Some winters it would be a woodwork class. He would always refuse to tell us ahead of time on what he was working, building his project up into a great mystery, especially for his children, and so it would always be a big event when, at the end of a term of instruction, he would bring home a finished product or two – an armchair, a coffee table, a bedside cabinet – all well made and sturdy, and some of which are still in use in my home today. Along with other miners he also attended St John Ambulance Brigade classes, where he learned about First Aid – how to give artificial respiration, how to make and apply a tourniquet, how to dress a wound, how to recognise different degrees of fractures, how to set a bone. He would take his turn at being available for well-attended public events – crowded football matches, carnivals or marches – dressed in the smart St John Ambulance Brigade peaked cap, black uniform with silver buttons, and wearing white gloves,

Many of the coal miners in our valley had come from cultured rural areas in the west, bringing along with them knowledge of poetry and literary skills. Others had come from coal-mining areas further east, and they were more knowledgeable about social and political issues, and economics. Some of them knew enough to teach others, and were willing, even eager, to share what they knew. Their fellow coal miners would, as it were, sit at their feet and learn from them, in informal classes held underground during meal breaks. In those days, coal mines could be academies as well as a tough work environment. It was from old hands who came from other coal mines to the east that Dad learned most, for his interest lay not in language and literature but in economic and social problems, and in political theory. When I became older I was surprised at how at home he was with those topics, and at the extent of his knowledge of them.

Dad's other goal in life was to be good. He was not during my childhood as faithful a chapelgoer as he was to become later, but already goodness in all its dimensions dominated his thinking and his choices. From the moment he left school, he lived and earned his living in a morally harsh environment, which was especially hard for such an overly conscientious person as he was. Near the footbridge which crossed the railway line to the main road, close to the flat in Jolly Road where I was born, there were railway sidings. Small locomotives sometimes brought wagons of coal in twos and threes from nearby collieries to those sidings, leaving the wagons there overnight, to be picked up all together the next morning by a larger locomotive and taken a further stage on their journey, to the docks in the town of Swansea, on the coast some 20 miles away.

More than once I heard Dad tell of an occasion or two when there was very little of his free coal ration left in our coal shed, when there was no money to buy any more, and when it was the depth of winter. Then he and my mother's brothers would go across to those sidings at night, to steal some coal from the wagons. One would climb up on to a wagon to throw lumps of coal down, two would stand below with sacks, ready to collect what was thrown down, and a fourth would keep watch some distance away – for the light of a torch which would be the sign that the local 'bobby', or policeman, was on the prowl. I doubt that it was possible to be more moral than Dad was; but he would always say that he would never admit to being ashamed of stealing that coal. One wonders, however, how the rest of his life would have turned out had he ever been caught and prosecuted, and how many of his kind there were to whom that happened.

Goodness for Dad meant many things. It meant being a good husband and father. That again he understood in terms of the black-and-white working class culture around him. In his father and father-in-law he had seen prime examples of both kinds. He knew which kind he didn't want to be, and he knew which kind he wanted to be. He made his choice and, as he did everything else, took his spousal and parental responsibilities very seriously.

His family was a priority. Many times, when he played games with my sister and me at the kitchen table on a chill winter's evening, or read stories to us at home in front of a grand fire, he was doing so not only to be the good father he wanted to be to us, he was also taking care of us so that Mam could take a rest, or enjoy a change – go out with a friend perhaps, to see a movie. On a Saturday afternoon, which most other men of his age regarded as a time when it was their masculine prerogative to play in a football or a cricket match, or to attend one as a spectator, Dad would walk with Mam, my sister and me to a park a mile or more further up the valley in Gwaun-Cae-Gurwen. He thought walking was 'good' for us all, and so he would encourage my sister and me to walk all the way there and back, but he always had a pushchair in front of him too, ready in case we really became too tired to walk. Then at the park he would join us on the roundabout, push us on the swings, watch over us as we climbed up one side of a slide, and wait for us at the bottom as we slid down the other side.

Like other coal miners of his type, he wanted his son not to have to go underground to earn a living, which meant getting a good education. He himself in fact didn't know enough about life's possibilities to dream great dreams for me. A secure job outside the mines was as big a dream as he was capable of.

But I sensed early in life that I had a father who wasn't going to be satisfied with doing what other acceptably good fathers around him were doing. He was determined to go beyond conventional patterns of good parenting. He wanted to be the very best father he had it in him to be, he aimed to excel quietly in this facet of life. Although reluctant in general to offer others, even his own son, advice (which made any piece of advice he gave that much more memorable), he would never shrink from advising or censuring me if he thought that he ought to do so. But more important than anything else was the spirit in which he advised or censured me. He always gave me space in which to be responsible for my own decisions, and he never scolded me without turning up at my bedside a minute or two before I fell asleep the same night to make sure I understood why he felt he had had to scold me, and to ensure we were still friends. Perhaps experiences of disrespect for his own person from which he had suffered as a child had made him ultra-sensitive to the rights even of young children, or possibly especially of young children.

He wanted me to know whatever he thought was appropriate for me to know at each stage in life, and never shirked that task, although his zeal sometimes took him beyond doing the right thing to the point of embarrassment for me. I wonder how many other fathers from his background in the Valleys in those days not only gave their teenage son a book to read called *How A Baby Is Born*, but took him aside after he had read it, looked him in the eye, and asked him whether he had any questions!

He also involved me as much as possible from my early

childhood in decisions affecting our life as a family. Every year, a week or so before Christmas, he would ask me whether I would accompany him to a nearby farm, Ffarm y Neuadd – which delivered milk to our doorstep every day – because, he would say, he needed my help in choosing a chicken for our Christmas dinner. After we had arrived at the farm, Dad would look for the farmer, Jack, and tell him our business. Jack would ask a few questions: 'Now, how many are you in the family, Dan? Do you want one just for Christmas Day or do you want it to last through Boxing Day too? I think one around 8 lb would do you fine then.' And we would walk around the farmyard, Jack pointing to various 8 lb-looking chickens roaming and scratching. 'That's a nice one there, Dan.' 'That one looks a little scrawny to me, Jack.' 'How about this one then?' 'Yes, I like the look of that one.' But Dad would not clinch the deal until he had turned to me and asked me for my opinion! 'What do you think? Will that one suit us?' And only after I had agreed would he tell Jack, 'Right then, we'll take that one.' They would shake hands, and the deal was done.

Early on Christmas Eve, Dad would take me back again to the farm, and into a cold, draughty barn with trestle tables at which women were plucking chickens. Jack would come over, ask someone where Dan Jones' chicken was, a woman would quickly look over the slips of paper pinned to the chickens already plucked and hanging, and in a moment she would cry out, 'Here it is, I'll wrap it up.' Before doing so she would show it to Dad, and we would make a quick check together to ensure as best we could that it was the one we had chosen that day out in the farmyard. Only then would Dad pay Jack, and home we would go with the chicken, which our womenfolk would inspect, and we would accept approval jointly.

Later in life, when I could see the unusual turns in some things he said, I was able to appreciate more fully not only the explicit, but also the implicit quality of fatherhood with which I had been blessed from birth. A good instance of the unusual way he sometimes thought was the time, after I had been married a few years, when he asked me one day what kind of a husband I was to Mary, my wife. It would have been an unexpected question from anyone, but it was especially unexpected from him, since he never presumed to intrude into anyone else's private life. I smiled and suggested that he ought to ask Mary, but his reply was simply that he was asking me. Even then I was tempted to make a jocular reply, but realising from the look on his face that a serious response was required, I said that I wanted to be a good husband, that I tried to be, and that as far as I knew I wasn't too bad a husband at least. Then I ventured to ask him with a grin whether he was going to ask Mary if she were a good wife to me. 'If I knew there were something wrong,' he replied, 'perhaps I might, but otherwise, my job is to make sure my children treat other people's children well.' It was a time in my marriage when the question of whether I was a good enough husband for my wife seemed to be more than adequately addressed by my in-laws, and so Dad's reply left me feeling somewhat beleaguered. I remember that that particular occasion led me to look back and to dwell on the fact that, although as a child I had always felt fully supported by him in all my conflicts with other children, and even with teachers, yet he always took time to lead me through any sense of injustice I experienced, and any resentment or anger I felt, to a view also of what might be going on in the mind of whoever I was having a problem with at the time.

Another instance of the way in which he thought was the importance for him of the concept of 'enough'. For one lengthy period in his life he was the secretary of the local branch of a trade union, and so was used to such realities as the rate for the job and wage bargaining. But it disappointed him when people he represented, regardless of what might be said openly in any wage negotiation, had within themselves no concept of what would satisfy them, other than that it should always be more. The idea of 'enough' for him had to do with the line between greed and appropriate demands – no matter how high the demand. For him, to have some idea of what was 'enough' for one in life had to do not only with essential personal satisfaction and well-being, but also with the quality of one's relationships with others. Toward the end of his working life he was a nurse at a hospital for older people, and he specialised in teaching people who had had a stroke how to walk again. Now and then, when approached by their families; he would give some of his spare time to help people who had had strokes and had been discharged from the hospital before they were quite ready to leave. But he always made it quite clear to those who sought his help in that way, and received it, that a condition of his doing it was that he should not receive payment. 'I get a fair salary at my place of work,' he would say, 'and it's enough.'

Raised at a time when families were large, in communities in which life was hard, and in a milieu in which there was little incentive to be demonstrative, meaning that signs of affection were virtually a discomfort, Mam and Dad were never able to express their love for me physically or verbally. I knew they loved me, but there was no hugging, no overt expressions of delight in me. As a result, much of my affection as a child for Dad too was expressed in secret, hidden ways. I would watch where, after working in the garden, he would put down the old, peaked cap he wore when gardening, and when his back was turned, I would pick it up, press its lining to my nose and inhale the strong, sweet, stale smell of male sweat. Later in life there were especially proud moments when I became old enough to use anything of his for the first time, often again in secret – his razor, his gardening clogs, an old jacket of his.

In the final analysis, Dad was for most of his life a stoic who could not believe that he was naturally entitled to any share of good fortune in this world. He had some hard evidence, for some of the cards had been stacked against him right from the beginning. When he turned 11, with the desire to learn already wide awake and alert in him, he was old enough now to sit an exam for a scholarship to the grammar school in the nearby town. But his mother told him that as his brother Rhys was also of an age to sit the exam, and as she wouldn't be able to afford the bus fare to school and to buy school books for two, it would be better for him not to sit the examination since, if both passed, it would be Rhys who would be allowed to attend the school, and so Dan would be disappointed. His father was a bystander in family matters, never interfering in decisions made by his mother, and so he didn't stand up for him either. It didn't help Dad then or later that while that first door in life had been slammed shut in his face in favour of his brother Rhys, Rhys himself (a morose male even by his own family's standards), who had never wanted to sit the exam and who didn't want to go to the grammar school, was disqualified during the exam for copying from another boy's paper.

Life had many more unnecessary and unjust traumas in store for him. In middle age, following a stint in the medical corps in the Royal Air Force in World War 2, he became a nurse, at a time when there were very few men in the profession. While women were fighting discrimination in traditionally male professions, he suffered discrimination in a traditionally female profession. He and his daughter both qualified as nurses within a few months of each other, but whereas she was promoted within two years, it took him fourteen to gain the same promotion. He came to feel that he had to earn even his right to be here, by sheer moral effort and integrity, and for most of his life he could never be sure in his heart that he was loved for himself. He was always struggling to understand grace, never quite losing the battle, yet never quite winning it either, until the very end of his life. He left his only son very little in the way of material goods, and nothing more valuable than an understanding of that lifelong, lonely, inner struggle.

A broad acquaintance with culture, the reading of certain novels perhaps, or an acquaintance with the work of some poets, might have given him a sense of community in hardship and injustice, and so might have eased the starkness of some of his more solitary and painful perceptions of life. But he never imbibed much in the way of culture, and never really took to art in any of its forms. Like most other people in the community around him, his aesthetic judgements were all strictly moral ones. Handel's Messiah was 'good', everyone knew that, and so if it were performed by some chapel choral society in the valley, he would go and listen to it, and would come home claiming it had made his hair stand on end, and what little hair he had might well have stood on end.

There was, of course, another side to that coin. I remember how sad and hurt I was, how separated and alienated from him I felt, when I met him one day after he had gone to see David Lean's movie version of Dr Zhivago, at my encouragement. He was angry: 'Why on earth did you tell me to go and see that film? If I want to know about adultery I can read about it in the newspaper every day, without paying good money to sit down and watch it for hours on end.'

Goodness for Dad also meant taking part in the political scene of his day. One of my early memories is of walking down the main street of our village on a Sunday afternoon, holding his hand, and surrounded by a great throng of men in procession. That day the Workmen's Hall was a forum for a speaker, and that speaker was James Griffiths, one of the earlier coal miners to aspire to become a Member of Parliament. He did become not only a Member of Parliament (in 1936), but as the first Minister for National Insurance and later Secretary of State for the Commonwealth in the Labour government which swept into power in 1946 in the aftermath of World War II, he also became a member of the Cabinet, and a politician respected on both sides of the House. His sons, notably pleasant and friendly boys, were later to become fellow-pupils of mine at Llanelli Grammar School. James Griffiths married an Englishwoman who was universally acclaimed and respected as a very fine person, but it was still a surprise to discover that the two sons of Jim Griffiths, a working class product of my valley and to his dying day a member of the Welsh-language chapel in whose graveyard he lies buried, weren't native Welsh speakers.

But again, the way people thought the wind was blowing in those days, and the way Welsh people thought about their own identity, there were many Welsh speakers who didn't consider Welsh much of a requirement, and didn't think it too big a deal not to pass on to their children the language they themselves had received through their parents. In contrast, and reflecting the changed times, one fairly recent Secretary of State for Wales who was an Englishman from Yorkshire began to learn Welsh, but since he eventually married his teacher we can't be absolutely sure that his motives were purely the product of a desire for cultural enlightenment!

The preachers and the chapel congregations of that time were ambivalent about the struggles of the miners. Some of the preachers became very active politically – one of the ministers of Bethel Newydd in Garnant eventually also became a Member of Parliament, and some chapels opened their doors to political gatherings. Some time ago Wales was given a second opportunity to vote on whether to have an Assembly of its own to administer Welsh affairs, and the vote this time, although very close, was positive. Today, the Welsh Assembly exists and is in operation. But as far back as 1885, Lloyd George, who became British Prime Minister during World War I, spoke from the pulpit of Bethel Newydd on the issue of Home Rule for Wales! Many chapel vestries served as soup kitchens for the local unemployed and their families during and after the General Strike of 1926.

Yet organised religion wasn't always helpful to working men concerned for their own rights and the rights of others. There was in some quarters a pious social and political inertia, and in others even a hostility which was critical of holding meetings that weren't overtly religious on a Sunday, and of attending union meetings which conflicted with weeknight activities in the chapel. Some too would contrast the 'worldly' struggle for better wages and working conditions with other-worldly spirituality. That side of the religious coin contributed at least something to the almost complete separation of the working class in Wales from the chapels in later years, but daily life and religion were all of a piece for Dad. He had no qualms about attending on a Sunday a political rally that couldn't be held on any other day.

I grew more and more aware even as a child of the great insecurities and hazards of coal mining, then in particular. Dad would sometimes be without work for weeks, and then get only a few days' work, or even a couple of half-shifts for a week or two. Getting a job was sometimes a matter of going to a colliery to see a manager and getting as close to begging him for employment as a man's pride would allow him.

Colliery managers had immense influence and power in their localities, and were of course a mix, like any other group of people. Sometimes a manager new to the district would join a local chapel, and his presence there could be divisive. At one extreme some would want to elect him a deacon or an elder immediately, thinking it an insult to him not to, or thinking that that would add to their chapel's prestige. At the other end were those who objected strongly to such action, which they considered to be subservience, and more so if the manager concerned were perceived by them to be in the pocket of the coal owners, and perhaps inhuman in his dealings with his workers. At least one manager I knew kept his membership in the chapel of his youth some distance away, while attending a chapel in the village in which he then lived and worked. He would give the chapel all the practical help he could, sending some of his workers along to help out with various labouring or technical jobs, but when he attended a service of worship there, he liked to arrive a little late, and he would always sit in an out-of-the-way place at the back of the chapel.

Dad was a man who had a very raw pride. He didn't find it easy to do anything that looked like begging for work. Work in his eyes was something a healthy man with family responsibilities who wanted work had a right to. During his longer periods of unemployment, he would occasionally go to ask a manager whether there was any work available, but that for him was an agonising task, and he would fret and fume in the house for hours on end before he went, as if he were somehow betraying a crucial part of his better self by going.

Added to the insecurity of employment were the great physical hazards of coal mining. Sometimes Dad would come home with his hand bandaged, a nail missing from one of his fingers perhaps. Once I was bundled out of the way as he was brought home in an ambulance, and two men, one on each side of him, carried him upright into the house. His face pale, his eyes staring, they supported him by holding him up under his armpits. As a child I was puzzled, since I could see no blood or bandage or any other sign of injury on him. That morning, I learned later, a cable pulling a number of trams full of coal up an incline underground had snapped, sending the trams careering backward down toward Dad. His only hope of saving his life had been to run for one of the small escape holes scattered here and there around the coal mine, and to dive headlong through it. To have failed would have been to be crushed to a pulp. It was the shock of raw fear that had made him unable to come home under his own steam that day, or even simply to stand up on his own feet without assistance.

For some miners, working deep in the bowels of the earth posed no problems – or even if it did to some extent, that was easily outweighed by their enjoyment of the camaraderie, and by the pride they took in what seemed to them to be the unequivocally male nature of their work. But for others, working underground day after day, week after week, month after month, year after year was psychologically stressful.

A coal miner's wife once told me that in a few weeks' time she was going for the first time to the United States, to take a holiday with a cousin of hers whom she had never met and who lived in Pennsylvania. I met her husband the next day and spoke to him.

'Are you packed and ready, Jack?'

'Packed and ready for what?'

'Packed and ready for your trip to the States, of course. Catherine tells me you're going there in a few weeks' time.'

'Oh, no. I'm not going. Catherine is going alone. She's going for a month, you see. It's not worth going that far for less than a month, is it? But I only have two weeks' holiday.'

'It's a shame not to go with her for the holiday of a lifetime, Jack – surely you can take two extra weeks off work without pay once in your life, for a special occasion?'

He paused a moment, looked carefully at me as if he were wondering whether or not to share something with me, then he lowered his voice and confided very quietly:

'You know, I get two weeks' holiday at the end of July every year, and at the end of those two weeks, going back underground again is almost more than I can bring myself to do. And it gets worse every year. If I were to be away for four weeks, I'm not sure I could ever go down there again. And what else would I do for a living? I don't know anything except coal mining. And I'm in my fifties, it's too late for me to learn any new tricks now.'

Some time later, at the invitation of a friend of mine who was a colliery manager, I went down a coal mine early one morning, and stayed there till the end of the day shift. Not all coal seams are the same thickness by any means – miners could work at some coal faces standing upright, but at one level I visited that day I traversed the 50 yards or so from one underground roadway to another, following a seam where the roof was so low that one could not even crawl along it on one's hands and knees, one had to strap leather pads to one's elbows and knees as a protection against the razor-sharp glass-like pieces of hard coal on the ground, then lie flat and propel oneself forward with one's elbows. Here and there I had to negotiate my way with some difficulty past miners whose job it was to work in there all day. Now and then, as I moved along, some small sound would make the miners stop almost imperceptibly in their work, and for a split second the lamp on my helmet would pick out the whites of their eyes as they instinctively glanced anxiously upwards.

Around the halfway mark, I was painfully aware of how far

I was from either roadway, and how far below the surface I was. I fell to thinking about the half-mile or so of earth above me, and of how little movement it might take for it to press downward without any warning at all just a couple of feet, snapping the wood or metal pit props which supported the roof as if they were matchsticks. Should that happen while I was there, it would surely be impossible for me, even were there some warning, to get out from where I lay except at a snail's pace, which would never be fast enough. Occasionally, that is how some miner would be killed, not by an explosion of gas or a sudden flood of water, or even a substantial collapse of the roof, but by being crushed, very, very slowly perhaps, pressure from above forcing a large rock downward a small distance of only two or three feet. I remember feeling a touch of panic, and trying to move faster along the last stretch of my crawl.

As I was leaving the mine that day, the trams (in one of which I was riding with several miners) rumbled steadily upward – this mine was a drift – pulled by a cable attached to the winch in the engine house on the surface. After a while I could see in the distance what seemed like the light of a small lamp. As it grew in size, I realised that what I was seeing was a small piece of sky. The light was daylight! As I realised how profoundly eager I was by then to emerge from depth and darkness into the world above, I sadly remembered Jack's words, and thought I understood them a little better.

Because, added to the dangers of the job, work for a young miner at that time was so very irregular, with the result that even enough income to buy life's bare necessities for a small family was hard to come by. Dad became increasingly convinced that coal mining wasn't appropriate work for a young husband and father. He believed a man should join with others to make great efforts to help create a rising economic and social tide that would lift all boats, but he also believed that a man had an individual responsibility for the well-being and the future of his own dependants.

He began looking around for alternative employment, and

eventually found a job in a village some 15 miles away, as an agent there for an insurance company. It entailed calling on people in their homes on a weekly basis to collect their contributions to whatever policy or policies they held with the insurance company, recording whatever their payments were in their own record books, entering them in the company's ledgers, and then banking the money. I sometimes wonder how many applied for that job. It was certainly a time of high unemployment in Wales – and in Britain for that matter. If many applied for it, why was Dad chosen? He wasn't an imposing presence by any means – he could walk into a room and you might never notice him. It was a job that required dependability and trust, of course. He would certainly be a good bet on both those counts. Perhaps there were those who spoke up for him. Perhaps his qualities were simply transparent to the man who would be his supervisor. I wish I had asked Dad before he died what his views were on the matter.

Comparatively late in life I was to make an occupational change that many others considered presented me with a very steep learning curve, but I more than suspect that when he changed his job, Dad's learning curve must have been a steeper one than mine. He went from shift work to regular hours; from going out every morning in a miner's dirty clothes to setting out in a white-collar worker's clean suit; from working the whole day in one fixed spot to cycling around streets and calling at many houses; from the physical work of handling pit ponies to the clerical work of handling a pen and figures and making entries in books; from dealing with fellow miners to dealing with mostly housewives, from leaving work at work to taking work home. I wish now we had talked long and hard before he died about that period of immense change in his life too, and how he coped. But make the change he did, successfully, and with that change we moved away from Garnant and the Amman Valley, the village and the valley in which I had been born and had spent my earlier years.

Dad went alone at first, lodging during the week with some

kind people who had been recommended to him, and returning home to us at weekends. He went to settle into his new job, and to find a suitable place for us to live together as a family. When he did find such a place, we joined him.

Although we didn't move a great distance, in many ways we entered a new and strange world. We lived now not in a valley, but on a coastal plain. We didn't own a car, and money wasn't too plentiful, so we couldn't often travel the two-stage bus ride back to the valley and the families and friends we had left, and we had no relatives at all in our new place of abode, although some uncommonly kind people befriended us. The local dialect was quite different to ours in some ways, which posed us some small problems for a while, and the nearest Congregational chapel, which was in the next village, was in that vicinity not the largest chapel, but the smallest, although in time that offered us a welcome intimacy.

My new school was bigger than the one I had left, and some of the boys and girls there were older than any of the boys and girls in my former school. The earliest memory I have of my new fellow pupils was of returning home at the end of my first day there and asking poor Dad the meaning of some obscene words that had been hurled abusively at me, and which I had never even heard before.

In my previous school I had found my place in the male pecking order uneventfully over time, and through many sporting activities – running, wrestling, jumping, playing marbles. But although fist fighting was a recognised male activity there, and an important enough activity for one boy to be the proven and acknowledged champion at it, in our class at least, I don't remember ever being involved in a fight myself. In my new school, from the standpoint of the other boys in my class, it was necessary that I should be located, correctly and quickly, in their pecking order. This was to be achieved simply by challenging me to engage in a series of fist fights.

I was small, but I was also sturdy, fast, and could give a good account of myself. However, in this matter I was handicapped.

To begin with, I had too vivid an imagination. I became anxious if I should hit another boy very hard, and I would then hesitate and hold back. I would want to stop and ask if he were alright before carrying on. I was also handicapped by a certain ambivalence. Dad had taught me the importance of standing up for myself, but he had also impressed on me that ultimately violence solved nothing. As a result of those two handicaps, I was able to beat boys bigger than me almost to submission, but I could never quite bring myself to deliver the punishing, decisive blow that those watching wanted to see and would accept as proof of superiority.

For others of life's battles, however, being the son of a coal miner – and of this particular coal miner, my father – has equipped me, I have always felt, better than anyone has a right to expect to be equipped.

CHAPTER 9

The Inheritance

ALTHOUGH DAD SPENT most of the latter part of his working life earning his living in other ways, he never forgot lessons learned and values gained through his early experience of being a coal miner. Those were guiding principles for him throughout his life. I too still think of myself, and want to think of myself, as a coal miner's son.

An upwardly-mobile and urbane Welshman living in the United States once upbraided me for mentioning in the company of some distinguished Americans that I had been born and spent my early years in a coal-mining valley and was born a coal miner's son. He was reflecting his own desire and even need perhaps for social approval, but in doing so, he was selling short something in the American psyche which approves of, for example, Abraham Lincoln's being born in a log-cabin and having worked as a rail-splitter. This attitude is distinctive of their society and to their very great credit, and is what has made the United States so congenial a home for many of its immigrants. My compatriot didn't seem to understand that I wasn't being careless or cavalier. I was acknowledging an integral part of my past, and not without pride, for I have always felt that in receiving my early upbringing in a coal mining valley, and as a coal miner's son in particular, I have received a goodly inheritance.

Many, as I have mentioned, have looked down on coal miners because of the nature of their work – carried out deep underground, some of it on their hands and knees, even on their elbows or lying on their sides, and leaving it at day's end looking unlike members of the human race. They have looked down on them too because of some of the rougher aspects of many coal-mining communities. Yet coal miners have also been acknowledged by many others to be a special breed.

There have been soldiers who might have been as courageous as some of their fellow soldiers who received commendations for valour in the face of the enemy, had they too been placed in situations which called for such bravery. So too there must have been workers in other industries who were implicitly as courageous as coal miners. But so much of the courage of coal miners has been very explicit.

There have been many, many instances of great individual bravery in coal mining. When I was a boy, Dad one day pointed out to me a man walking by. He was middle-aged and squat, an unlikely-looking hero, whose name I know now was Idris. 'Take a good look at that man,' said Dad, in one of those rare, formal statements he made from time to time, 'because that man deserves your admiration and respect.' He went on to explain. Many years previously, when Idris had been a young man, there had been a gas explosion underground in one of the Amman Valley's coal mines. The explosion had brought down the roof of the mine at the place where it had occurred, and three men who had been working the seam just beyond that point were trapped behind the fall. The manager of the mine had no means of knowing how the three men might have fared, but he feared that there was still more gas around in that section of the seam. He knew that only one spark from the blow of a pick against a stone, in an attempt to remove the rocks and rubble behind which the men were trapped, would be all it would take to cause another explosion. Unwilling to expose any more men to the risk of great danger, he had made the agonising decision to forbid any rescue attempt as yet. But Idris, in defiance of the manager's orders, had dashed alone into that section of the seam, had clawed through the debris with his bare hands, and had eventually managed to carry out each of the three men to where others could reach them, stunned and badly burned, but alive.

A communal courage also developed among these men who earned their living always in the presence of great danger. A doctor in one coal-mining community who deserves to be named and so remembered, Dr D Aubrey Thomas of Dyffryn Cellwen, describing on the radio an occasion when he had to go below ground to rescue a miner whose leg had got caught in a coal-cutting machine, said of coal miners, 'Of course the amazing thing about it is that the very next morning, in cold blood, they go back into a place where the same thing can well happen... They're not sort of keyed up to it by the knowledge that it will, in the sense of a man going over the top in a battle or anything like that, but are dogged by the knowledge that it might all the time; and it's this cold-blooded heroism that you get among miners. These people go down after a cold breakfast early in the morning in the winter, to the same set of circumstances, and they just go on with it.' It was a heroism that their womenfolk, their mothers, wives, daughters and sisters, shared in a different way.

Coal miners have also been in the vanguard in the industrial and political struggle for social justice in Britain. In the late 1940s, 1950s and 1960s, before the deep-mining coal industry was dismantled, the coal-mining communities of South Wales, along with coal-mining communities elsewhere in Britain, managed to achieve most of what they had long demanded and fought for – decent wages, good healthcare, sound safety systems, and fair compensation for injury. Pithead facilities were also built for them, locker rooms and showers, so they could go to work in clean clothes and return home at the end of a shift not only in clean clothes, but also now with clean bodies, clean hands, and clean faces that could be recognised. Those pithead facilities made an immense change for the coal miners themselves, not only in practice but in self-esteem. It meant they could travel home with others on regular bus services should they need to, or even just want to, and not be forever segregated on ancient, filthy buses laid on especially for coal miners. It made a difference to their homes and their families too, especially their wives of course, for now the coal miners brought none of the colliery's grime and dirt home with them – it was all left where it ought to be left, at the pithead. The coal miners had finally succeeded in building – although it was to last for only a very limited time – the kind of communities Tad-cu could only have dreamed of, and what one of their own historians has even called 'citadels of the spirit'.

It had been a great venture, and through it coal miners, as a group, learned two things above all. They learned about strong solidarity. In their daily work they depended on each other for their very lives. That doctor who spoke on the radio of the heroism of coal miners, spoke of that solidarity too, in reference to the same occasion. 'What one's impressed with in a scene like that is just the readiness of help, you know the roof's all falling in... and although the posts keep knocking out, you had an embarrassment of help... It really makes you realise what grand guys these people are... No danger keeps them away from an injured man... it doesn't matter what risk it is to them... and they all have the same sort of feeling, it's a sort of *esprit de corps* that you get underground – you never meet with it anywhere else; I've never met with it anywhere in the world.'

Socially also, the coal miners depended on each other in the industrial and political battle for their rights. They knew solidarity with other beleaguered groups too, for their struggle was not for themselves and theirs alone. They raised money and marched, they stood up to be counted, on behalf of workers in other industries elsewhere. They contributed greatly to changing for the better, to humanising, the face of the Britain of their day. A contingent of them even left South Wales to fight, some of them to die, in the struggle against fascism in Spain in the 1930s. Dad never forgot that for a time he had been a part of that whole great venture.

I have had friends, some of them close friends, who were sons of teachers, shopkeepers or ministers and who during childhood enjoyed many privileges denied to me. Yet I have more than once felt that I have not been as close to, not had as deep a relationship with, not enjoyed as strong a bond of loyalty with some of them as I would have wished. There have even been times, it seems to me, when some of them seem to have trivialised some substantial experience we have undergone together. I have often wondered at such times whether they, in not being close in their early lives to a father – and a grandfather – and to communities for whom solidarity with others was a paramount daily experience, have been deprived of a privilege that would have enabled them to enjoy a more in-depth engagement with society.

Coal miners also learned about the view of life from below in more than the literal sense. A view of life from below is, of course, not the greatest of handicaps to understanding many of the forces which are right now changing the face of our world, from respect for minorities, to the writing of history, to the nature and disposition of power.

As a student at an American college in the late sixties and early seventies, the time of the death of Martin Luther King, the moon landing, the Vietnam War and the burning of draft cards, and the shooting of black students by the National Guard at Kent State University, a crucial and formative time in America in general, but more especially on college campuses, I would often listen to a dispute between a white student and a black student. On some of those occasions it would seem to me that the white student was completely failing to understand what the black student was saying. Once or twice I ventured to try and explain to the white student, 'I think what he means is...' And should the black student nod his head in agreement, I knew it was the coal miner's son in me that had got it right.

Although I have by this time lived for more years outside a valley than within a valley, I also still think of myself as a valley person. I began this volume by quoting a Welsh poet who wrote in Welsh. T H Parry-Williams, another Welsh poet who wrote in Welsh was born and raised within sight of Snowdon, the highest mountain in Wales. He too left the place of his early childhood at a young age, but years later as a mature adult he confessed to still feeling lost, dispersed, confused even, in flat terrain, whereas if there were a mountain somewhere in sight he knew exactly who he was.

After I had lived once for six months in the wonderful but flat state of Minnesota in the US, one autumn evening some friends of mine, a married couple, took me by car from the city of Minneapolis to a small town in Wisconsin. We were on the way to dinner at the house of friends of theirs there. First we made for Stillwater, a very distinctive old town of great character, some 30 minutes' drive away from Minneapolis, and where the first meeting to discuss statehood for Minnesota was held. From Stillwater we crossed the steel bridge over the broad St Croix River, just a few miles from where it joins the Mississippi, and entered Wisconsin. I was sitting alone in the back of the car. It was dusk when we had begun our journey, but by this time it was dark. A few seconds after we entered Wisconsin, there emerged from me what must have sounded like a long moan. For a few moments my friends thought that I had been taken ill. The driver slowed down. His wife asked me if I were alright. I laughed with embarrassment. My moan had really been a sigh, a deep sigh, of relief. For the first time in months I was in a car in which the bonnet was high enough above the boot so that I was tipped backward in my seat. On the road entering Wisconsin from the bridge over the St Croix at Stillwater, Minnesota, I was, I realised, on the side of a valley. For the first time in quite a while, this particular Welshman in the US of A knew again exactly who he was.